AF481637

Cedar Point PALETTE

A Gallery of Southern Recipes

Girl Scouts of Northwest Mississippi

CEDAR POINT PALETTE

A Gallery of Southern Recipes

Girl Scout Council of Northwest Mississippi, Inc.

Copyright © 2003 by
Girl Scout Council of Northwest Mississippi, Inc.
305 East Washington, Greenwood, MS 38930
662-453-2034
mcates@girlscoutsnwms.org

This cookbook is a collection of favorite recipes,
which are not necessarily original recipes.

ISBN: 0-9742396-0-7

Edited, Designed, and Manufactured by

CommunityClassics™
An imprint of

FRP

P.O. Box 305142
Nashville, Tennessee 37230
800-358-0560

Manufactured in the United States of America
First Printing: 2003
Number of copies: 5000

Dedication

Our Girl Scout camp, Cedar Point, is highlighted in this cookbook because so many girls and women throughout the South have made wonderful memories and friends here on Grenada Lake.

The Girl Scout Council of Northwest Mississippi stretches over seventeen counties in the heart of the Delta. The primary focus of the Council is to reach "Every Girl Every Where." By purchasing this cookbook, you will assist in this endeavor.

The goal in creating *Cedar Point Palette* is to highlight special recipes for all occasions and lifestyles and to acknowledge the many volunteers and girls who contributed them.

Gratitude is expressed to the Staff of the Council for their dedication and work in bringing this culinary experience to you. A special thanks is extended to Evelyn North for editing this work.

An attempt was made to use all recipes submitted, and we regret if there are any errors or omissions.

A United Way Agency

Contents

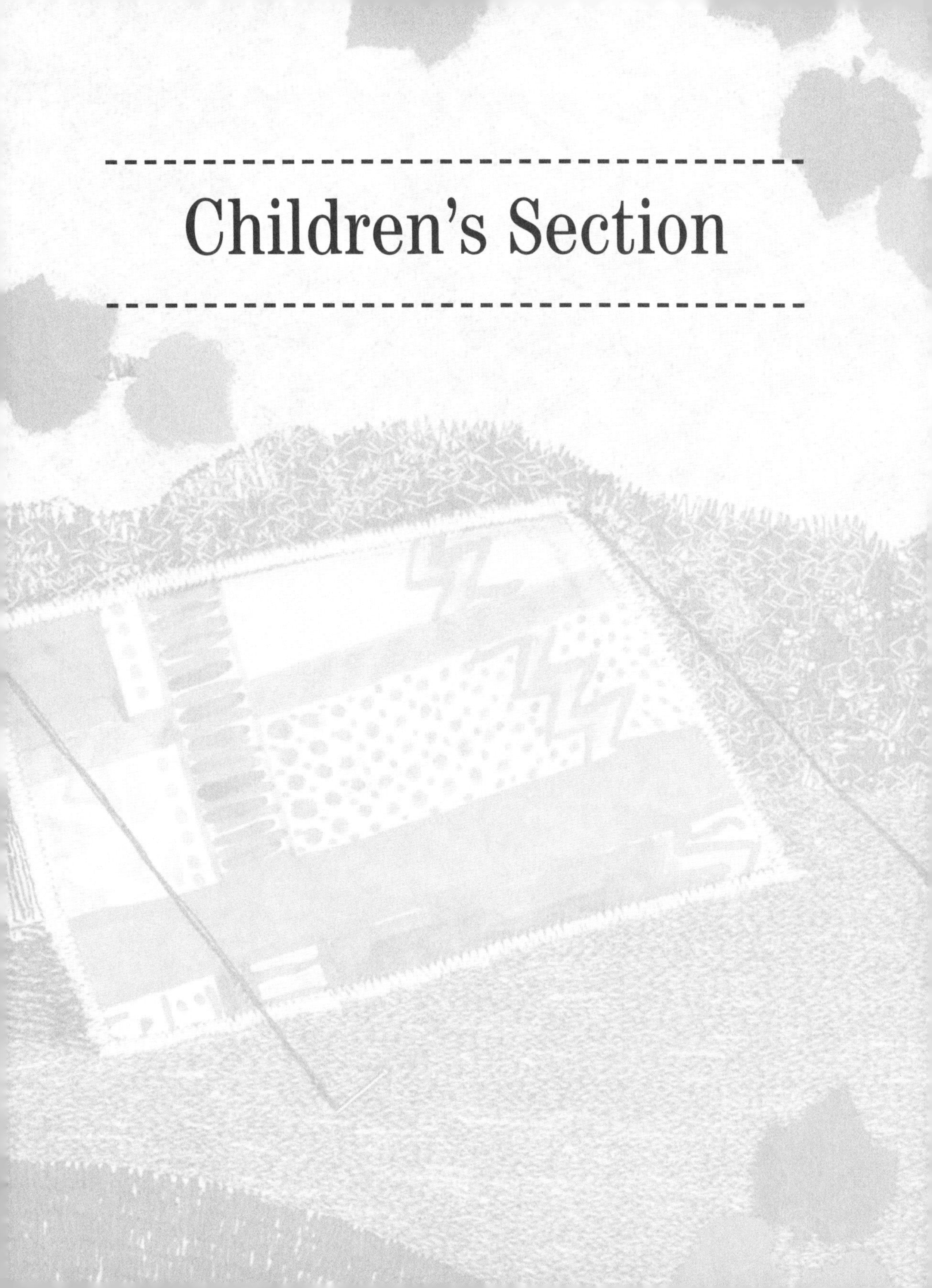

Children's Section

Children's Recipes

Indoor and Outdoor Fun

Here are a few easy recipes for tried-and-true children's activities. The soap bubbles are best for outdoors but could be done from a porch or other sheltered area even when it's raining.

Soap Bubbles

Combine 2 cups warm water, 2 tablespoons liquid detergent, 1 tablespoon sugar and 1 tablespoon glycerin in a shallow bowl. The glycerin is optional but it will make the bubbles iridescent. Blow the bubbles through a wire loop or spool. To make lots of bubbles at once, try dipping a fly swatter in the soapy liquid and swinging it through the air.

No-Cook Play Dough

Combine 1 cup flour and 1 cup salt in a mixing bowl. Stir in 1 tablespoon vegetable oil. Add drops of food coloring to a small amount of water and stir just enough of the water into the flour mixture to make a dough consistency.

Finger Paint

Spoon dry tempera colors into small bowls or plastic containers. Stir in enough liquid detergent or liquid starch to make a paint consistency.

Popcorn Balls

1 (14-ounce) package caramels
1/4 cup corn syrup
2 tablespoons water
2 1/2 quarts popped popcorn, kept warm in a
200-degree oven

Place the caramels in a large microwave-safe bowl. Microwave on High for 1 minute or until melted. Add the corn syrup and water and stir until smooth. Pour the mixture slowly over the popped corn in a large mixing bowl or pan, stirring constantly until the popcorn is evenly coated.

Shape the mixture with greased hands into softball-size balls. Let stand until cool and dry. Wrap tightly in plastic wrap.

Yield: 10 to 12 popcorn balls

Nancy Jackson, Product Sales Manager

Girl Scout Trivia
In 1912, Juliette Gordon Low started the first Girl Scout troop in Savannah, Georgia. Daisy Gordon, her niece, was the first registered member.

Granny Goose Popcorn

1 bag microwave popcorn
1 cup sugar
1/4 cup (1/2 stick) butter
3 tablespoons water
1 tablespoon vanilla extract

Microwave the popcorn using the package directions. Combine the sugar, butter and water in a saucepan. Cook over high heat until bubbly. Stir in the vanilla. Pour over the popcorn in a baking dish and stir well. Bake at 250 degrees until the mixture begins to dry out, stirring occasionally.

Yield: 4 to 5 servings

Suzy McCrimmon, Troop #275

Microwave Popcorn

1 bag microwave popcorn

Microwave the popcorn on High for 4 1/2 to 5 minutes or use the package directions. Open and serve immediately.

Yield: 1 to 2 servings

Karrissa Smith, Troop #233

Easy Bake Oven Brownies

1 package Easy Bake Oven brownie mix
1 batter spoonful (1 teaspoon) water

Combine the brownie mix and water in a small mixing bowl. Spread the mixture in a greased Easy Bake Oven pan. Push the pan into the oven using the Easy Bake Oven tool. Bake for 20 minutes. Pull the pan out of the oven using the tool. Let cool.

Yield: 1 serving

Morgan Young, Troop #7

Girl Scout Trivia
You don't have to live in America to be a member of the Girl Scouts. U.S.A. Girl Scouts Overseas forms troops in foreign counries where Americans work in embassies, the oil industry, and the U.S. armed forces. The organization currently serves more than 23,000 girls in eighty-one countries.

S'mores

Peanut butter
Graham crackers
Milk chocolate bars
Large marshmallows, roasted

Spread the peanut butter on one side of a graham cracker square. Top with a square of chocolate, a hot marshmallow and another graham cracker square. Press the graham crackers together gently.

Yield: variable

Shyandrea S. Glass, Troop #234

Frozen Cookies

1 package frozen cookies

Place the cookies on a greased cookie sheet. Bake at 375 degrees for 10 to 12 minutes. Cool on a wire rack for 5 minutes.

Yield: variable

Shenita Williams, Troop #233

Magic Cookie Bars

1/2 cup (1 stick) butter or margarine
1¹/2 cups graham cracker crumbs
1 (14-ounce) can sweetened condensed milk
2 cups (12 ounces) semisweet chocolate chips
1¹/3 cups flaked coconut
1 cup chopped walnuts
1 cup dried cranberries (optional)

Melt the butter in a 9×13-inch baking pan in a 350-degree oven. Layer the graham cracker crumbs, condensed milk, chocolate chips, coconut, walnuts and cranberries over the butter. Press the layers firmly with a fork.

Bake at 350 degrees for 25 minutes or until light brown. Let stand until cool. Chill, if desired, before cutting. Cut into bars or diamonds. Store the bars at room temperature.

Yield: 24 to 36 bars

Note: Substitute candy-coated chocolate pieces, raisins, miniature marshmallows or butterscotch chips for the chocolate chips or nuts.

Kiara Swinney, Troop #259

Crispy Treats

1 (10-ounce) bag marshmallows
3 tablespoons margarine or butter
6 cups crisp rice cereal

Melt the marshmallows and margarine in a saucepan over low heat. Add the cereal and stir until well coated. Spread the mixture in a greased 9×13-inch baking dish. Let stand until cool. Cut into squares.

Yield: 12 to 16 squares.

Chef Christee, Troop #29

Girl Scout Trivia
The first troop members were called Girl Guides like the group in England. The following year, the name was changed to Girl Scouts.

Peanutty Monster Mix

1/4 cup peanut butter
1/4 cup (1/2 stick) margarine
5 cups Crispix cereal
2 cups small pretzel twists or rings
1/2 cup Spanish peanuts
1 cup candy-coated milk chocolate pieces, small
    gumdrops or gummi candies
1 cup raisins

Combine the peanut butter and margarine in a large microwave-safe bowl. Microwave on High for 30 seconds or until the margarine is melted. Stir until smooth. Add the Crispix cereal, pretzels and peanuts and stir gently until evenly coated. Microwave on High for 3 minutes longer, stirring after each minute. Spread on paper towels to cool. Remove to a large mixing bowl and stir in the candy and raisins. Store in an airtight container.

Yield: 16 servings

Nyteshia Jones, Troop #25

Trail Mix

3 (14-ounce) packages granola
1 (24-ounce) package raisins
1 (16-ounce) can mixed nuts
1 (14-ounce) bag "M & M's" Chocolate Candies

Combine the granola, raisins, nuts and "M & M's" Chocolate Candies in a large mixing bowl. Store in an airtight container.

Yield: 20 to 30 servings

Note: Vary the ingredients according to the occasion. For example, use seasonal "M & M's" for Christmas or Easter. For a study of Africa, use animal crackers, banana chips and regular "M & M's" to match the colors of kente cloth. For a tropical theme, add dried fruits such as pineapple, dates and coconut; or in teaching about Johnny Appleseed, use only red "M & M's" and add apple chips. Use your imagination.

Margaret Anne Mitchell, former trainer

Caramel Apples

12 caramel slices, at room temperature
12 large apples, washed
Chopped peanuts

Wrap a caramel slice around each apple. Roll the apples in the peanuts until evenly coated. Insert a popsicle stick into the bottom center of each apple.

Yield: 12 servings

Shatez Scott, Troop #29

Hiking Apples

1 large apple
Peanut butter
Jelly

Insert a knife or apple corer into the stem end of the apple; remove the core, leaving the bottom of the apple intact. Drop spoonfuls of peanut butter and jelly alternately into the apple. Place in a sealable plastic bag and take along on a day hike.

Yield: 1 serving

Rebecca Koehler, Daisy Scout

Egg and Cheese Sandwich

2 eggs, beaten
Salt and pepper to taste
2 slices white bread, toasted
1 slice American cheese
1 slice Swiss cheese

Beat the eggs with salt and pepper in a small bowl. Cook in a hot skillet coated with nonstick cooking spray, stirring constantly until done to taste. Top each slice of toast with a slice of cheese and half of the eggs. Combine the two slices into a sandwich and cut in half.

Yield: 1 serving

Benekia Wilkins, Troop #233

Toast and Jelly

2 slices wheat bread, toasted
1 tablespoon grape jelly

Spread each slice of hot toast with the jelly.

Yield: 1 to 2 servings

Arielle Bush, Troop #233

Toad-in-a-Hole

1 slice bread
Butter, softened
1 egg

Cut a circle from the middle of the bread slice, using a cookie cutter. Spread butter on both sides of the bread slice. Melt 1 tablespoon butter in a skillet over medium heat. Place the bread slice in the skillet. Break the egg into a saucer and pour the egg into the hole in the bread. Cook until the egg is firm. Serve immediately.

Yield: 1 serving

Nancy Jackson, Product Sales Manager

Guadalupe Chili Pie

2 pounds ground beef
1 medium onion, chopped
1 tablespoon margarine
1 (15-ounce) can chili beans
1/2 teaspoon chili powder
1/2 teaspoon salt
1 (8-ounce) can tomato sauce
1 (6-ounce) package corn bread mix

Brown the ground beef with the onion and margarine in a Dutch oven, stirring until the ground beef is crumbly; drain. Add the chili beans, chili powder, salt and tomato sauce. Cook, covered, for 15 minutes. Prepare the corn bread mix using the package directions. Spread over the ground beef mixture. Place a large piece of foil on the ground. Arrange 6 to 8 hot charcoal briquettes in the center and set the covered Dutch oven on top of the briquettes. Bring the foil up and around the Dutch oven to entirely cover it. Place another 15 to 18 hot briquettes on top of the Dutch oven. Cook for 20 to 30 minutes or until the corn bread is done.

Yield: 8 servings

Sarah Koehler, Troop #298

Piggy Blankets

1 (8-count) can crescent rolls
1 package cocktail franks

Separate the crescent rolls and cut each triangle into three narrow wedges. Place a cocktail frank on each wedge and roll up the wedges from the wide ends. Bake at 325 degrees until golden brown.

Yield: 24 appetizers

Layla Taylor, Troop #270

Hot Dog

2 hot dogs
2 hot dog buns

Bring enough water to cover the hot dogs to a boil in a saucepan. Add the hot dogs. Cook for 5 minutes; drain. Place a hot dog in each bun.

Yield: 2 servings

Lakittra Smith, Troop #233

Hot Dogs and Crescents

1 3/4 cups baking mix
1/3 cup milk
1 tablespoon prepared mustard
3 tablespoons pickle relish, drained
2 slices American cheese, cut into strips
8 hot dogs

Combine the baking mix, milk and prepared mustard in a mixing bowl; stir to make a soft dough. Beat with a wooden spoon for 30 seconds. Remove the dough to a surface sprinkled with additional baking mix. Roll the dough in the mix to coat well. Shape the dough into a ball and knead 10 times. Pat into a 13-inch circle. Cut into 8 wedges. Place 1 teaspoon of the pickle relish and 1 strip of the cheese on each wedge about 1 inch from the rounded edge. Place a hot dog in the center of each wedge and roll up the wedges from the wide ends. Place on a greased baking sheet. Bake at 425 degrees for 12 minutes or until golden brown.

Yield: 8 servings

Jasmine Roberts, Troop #170

Ham and Cheese Sandwich

2 slices wheat bread
1/2 teaspoon mayonnaise
1/2 teaspoon prepared mustard
2 slices deli ham
1 slice American cheese
1 slice Swiss cheese

Spread the bread slices with the mayonnaise and mustard. Layer the ham, American cheese and Swiss cheese on one slice of the bread. Top with the second slice of bread. Cut the sandwich in half.

Yield: 1 serving

Markecia Hampton, Troop #223

Fried Bologna Sandwich

2 slices bologna
1 teaspoon butter or margarine
2 slices bread

Cook the bologna in the butter in a small skillet until it is hot and browned. Sandwich the bologna between the bread slices. Cut the sandwich in half.

Yield: 1 serving

Rolecia Johnson, Troop #233

Turkey and Swiss Cheese Sandwich

2 slices wheat bread
Mayonnaise (optional)
3 slices deli turkey
2 slices Swiss cheese

Spread the bread slices with the mayonnaise. Layer the turkey and cheese on one slice of the bread. Top with the second slice of bread. Cut the sandwich in half.

Yield: 1 serving

Chiquita Green, Troop #233

BLT (Bacon, Lettuce and Tomato Sandwich)

2 slices white bread, toasted
1/2 teaspoon mayonnaise
4 slices bacon, crisp-cooked and drained
4 thin slices tomato
1 lettuce leaf

Spread the bread slices with the mayonnaise. Layer the bacon, tomato and lettuce on one slice of the bread. Top with the second slice of bread. Cut the sandwich in half.

Yield: 1 serving

Karly Lester, Troop #233

Crunchy Peanut Butter and Jelly Sandwich

2 slices white bread
1 tablespoon crunchy peanut butter
1 tablespoon grape jelly

Spread one slice of the bread with the peanut butter. Spread the jelly over the peanut butter. Top with the second slice of bread. Cut the sandwich in half and serve with a glass of milk.

Yield: 1 serving

Antwaia Baker, Troop #233

Peanut Butter and Crackers

Crackers
Peanut butter

Place the crackers on a paper towel. Spread the crackers with the peanut butter. Top each with another cracker. Serve with a glass of water.

Yield: variable

Keitasha Kennedy, Troop #233

Noodles

4 cups water
1/2 teaspoon garlic powder
1 package beef ramen noodles
1 package mushroom ramen noodles
1/3 cup chopped green onions
2 teaspoons soy sauce

Bring the water to a boil in a saucepan. Add the garlic powder, beef ramen noodles and mushroom ramen noodles. Cook until the noodles are tender; drain 1/2 of the water.

Stir in the contents of the noodle seasoning packets, green onions and soy sauce. Mix well and let stand for 2 minutes.

Yield: 2 servings

Alesha Briscoe, Troop #259

Waldorf Salad for a Troop

10 apples
5 bananas
**1 (16-ounce) package chopped pecans or
walnuts**
1 (4-ounce) jar mayonnaise

Peel the apples or leave them unpeeled, as desired. Core and seed the apples and cut them into bite-size pieces. Place the apples in a large salad bowl. Slice the bananas into the bowl and add the pecans. Add the mayonnaise and stir until the fruit is evenly coated. Chill the salad until ready to serve.

Yield: 20 or more servings

Note: You can adjust all the proportions of the ingredients in this salad to suit your own family's taste. This is an easy recipe to make while camping.

Rebecca Koehler, Daisy Scout

Slap Yo Mama Salsa

1 cup cooked rice
1 (15-ounce) can black-eyed peas with
jalapeño chiles, drained and washed
1 garlic clove, minced
1 (10-ounce) can tomatoes with green chiles
1/2 cup chopped red onion
1/2 cup chopped green bell pepper
1/2 cup chopped red bell pepper (optional)
1 (8-ounce) can niblet corn, drained
1 (8-ounce) bottle hot pepper sauce
3 tablespoons vegetable oil (optional)

Combine the rice, black-eyed peas, garlic, tomatoes with green chiles, red onion, bell pepper and niblet corn in a large serving bowl. Drain the liquid from the hot pepper sauce into the rice and vegetable mixture, leaving the hot peppers in the bottle. Add the oil. Stir the salsa. Chill overnight. Serve with rice crackers or other favorite crackers.

Yield: 15 to 20 appetizer servings

Sarah Koehler, Troop #298

Appetizers

How Many Appetizers Should I Make?

When planning a dinner or cocktail party, you may often find yourself wondering how many appetizers to plan per person. Here are some tips from Cheryl Brown of *Gourmet* magazine.

For a cocktail party, figure twelve pieces per person times the number of people divided by the number of different appetizers. (When they are being served before a full dinner, halve the total.)

If the guest list has fewer than forty-five people, plan on using roughly six different appetizers; for more than forty-five guests, eight types. The rule of thumb for smaller gatherings is that three types are suitable for eight to ten guests; four or five for fourteen to sixteen people.

Having an equal number of hot and cold foods is also helpful so that while one appetizer is heating in the oven, a cold one can be circulating, keeping everyone nibbling happily.

Pink Grapefruit Sparkle

1 cup water
3/4 cup frozen grapefruit juice concentrate, thawed
3/4 cup frozen lemonade concentrate, thawed
3 tablespoons grenadine
1 (1-liter) bottle carbonated water, chilled

Combine the water, grapefruit juice concentrate, lemonade concentrate and grenadine in a 2-quart pitcher and mix well.

Cover and chill until serving time. Stir in the carbonated water just before serving. Serve over ice.

Yield: 8 servings

Pam Cornacchione, Troop #115

Bride's Pink Punch

1 (3-ounce) package strawberry-flavored gelatin
1 cup boiling water
1 (2-quart) envelope strawberry-flavored drink mix
2 quarts cold water
2 1/2 cups sugar
1 (46-ounce) can pineapple juice
1 (10-ounce) bottle lemon-lime soda
2 pints pineapple sherbet

Dissolve the gelatin in the boiling water in a small bowl. Dissolve the drink mix in the cold water in a large container. Add the sugar and mix well. Add the pineapple juice and the dissolved gelatin mixture. Chill until serving time. Pour into a punch bowl. Stir in the lemon-lime soda and sherbet just before serving.

Yield: 30 servings

Nancy Jackson, Product Sales Manager

Country Lemonade

1 cup sugar
1 cup boiling water
1¹/₃ cups fresh lemon juice (6 to 7 lemons)
Lemon zest to taste

Dissolve the sugar in the boiling water in a 1-quart pitcher. Cool to room temperature. Add the lemon juice, lemon zest and enough water to fill the pitcher; mix well.

Chill until serving time. Serve over ice in tall glasses and garnish with lemon slices.

Yield: 8 servings

LaShondria Gooden, Troop #252

Frosted Orange Drink

1 (6-ounce) can frozen orange juice concentrate
1/2 cup sugar
1 cup water
1 cup milk
1 teaspoon vanilla extract

Combine the orange juice concentrate, sugar, water, milk and vanilla in a blender. Add crushed ice to fill the blender. Process until the mixture is slushy and the outside of the container is frosted. Serve immediately in stemmed glasses.

Yield: 4 servings

Danisha Wilson Williams, Troop #252

Black Cow

2 scoops vanilla ice cream
1 (12-ounce) can cola

Place the vanilla ice cream in a tall glass. Fill the glass with cola and stir until slushy.

Yield: 1 serving

Kenisha Orsby, Troop #252

Raspberry Punch

1 pint raspberry sherbet
1 quart ginger ale

Scoop the raspberry sherbet into a punch bowl. Pour the ginger ale over the sherbet.

Yield: 10 servings

Mary Alice Cates, Executive Director

Party Punch

1 (46-ounce) can pineapple juice
1 1/2 cups sugar
1 (8-ounce) bottle lemon juice
1 (12-ounce) can frozen orange juice concentrate
1 (2-liter bottle) ginger ale

Pour some of the pineapple juice into an ice cube tray and freeze. Combine the remaining pineapple juice, sugar, lemon juice, orange juice concentrate, ginger ale and 1 juice can water in a punch bowl. Float the frozen pineapple juice cubes in the bowl.

Yield: 25 servings

Mary Alice Cates, Executive Director

Coca-Cola Punch

Juice of 12 lemons
Grated zest of 1 lemon
1 cup sugar
36 ounces Coca-Cola

Combine the lemon juice, lemon zest and sugar in a bowl. Let stand for 10 to 12 hours. Add the Coca-Cola and pour over crushed ice in a punch bowl just before serving.

Yield: 8 servings

Council Recipe

Girl Scout Trivia
There are 109 proficiency badges available to Junior Girl Scouts and sixty-six Interest Project patches for Girl Scouts.

Homemade Tomato Juice

**10 to 12 large tomatoes, cored and blossom ends
    removed
1 teaspoon salt
1 teaspoon seasoned salt
1/4 teaspoon pepper
1 tablespoon sugar**

Bring a large pot of water to a boil. Add the tomatoes. Cook for
8 to 10 minutes or until the tomatoes are soft; drain. Press through
a sieve or food mill into a large container, discarding the skins and
seeds. Stir in the salt, seasoned salt, pepper and sugar. Chill until
serving time.

Yield: 6 to 8 servings

Sherry Kelly, Communications Director

Hot Chocolate Mix

1 (8-quart) package dry milk powder

1 (16-ounce) package chocolate drink mix

2 cups confectioners' sugar

8 ounces dry nondairy coffee creamer

Combine all the ingredients in a large container and mix well. Cover tightly and store. For 1 serving: spoon $3^{1}/_{2}$ teaspoons of the mix into a mug. Pour 1 cup hot water over the mix and stir well.

Yield: 100 servings

Nancy Jackson, Product Sales Manager

Hot Spiced Tea

4 cups water

16 whole cloves

2 cinnamon sticks

1 (12-ounce) can frozen orange juice

$2^{1}/_{2}$ cups sugar

1 (12-ounce) can frozen lemonade

12 cups weak brewed tea

Bring the water to a boil in a saucepan. Add the cloves and cinnamon sticks. Cook for 5 to 10 minutes. Combine the remaining ingredients in a large saucepan. Strain the clove and cinnamon stick mixture into the tea mixture and stir well. Heat the entire mixture in the large saucepan for a large group or store the mixture in the refrigerator and heat individual servings as needed.

Yield: 25 to 30 servings

Annie Roby, Field Executive

Slow-Cooker Broccoli Cheese

1 cup chopped celery
1/2 cup chopped onion
**1 (10-ounce) package frozen chopped
    broccoli, cooked and drained**
1 cup cooked rice
1 (10-ounce) can cream of mushroom soup
**1 (16-ounce) jar cheese spread, or 15 slices
    American cheese, melted and mixed
    with 2/3 cup milk**

Combine the celery, onion, broccoli, rice, cream of mushroom soup and cheese spread in a slow cooker. Cook on Low for 2 hours. Serve with snack breads or crackers.

Yield: 20 to 25 servings

Annie Roby, Field Executive

The Girl Scout Promise Made by Girls and Adults
On my honor, I will try:
To serve God and my country,
To help people at all times,
And to live by the Girl Scout law.

Hot Broccoli Dip

1 medium onion, chopped
1/4 cup (1/2 stick) margarine
2 (10-ounce) packages frozen chopped broccoli,
   cooked and drained
1 (10-ounce) can cream of mushroom soup
1 (4-ounce) can chopped mushrooms, drained
1 (6-ounce) roll garlic cheese

Cook the onion in the margarine in a skillet until tender. Add the broccoli, cream of mushroom soup, mushrooms and garlic cheese.

Heat until the cheese is melted, stirring constantly. Remove the dip to a chafing dish and serve hot with crackers or corn chips.

Yield: 10 servings

Council Recipe

Corn Dip

2 (11-ounce) cans Mexican-style corn, drained
1 (4-ounce) can chopped green chiles
1½ cups (6 ounces) shredded Cheddar cheese
1 cup mayonnaise
1 cup sour cream
5 or 6 green onions, chopped
Pepper to taste
Cajun seasoning to taste (optional)

Combine the corn, green chiles, cheese, mayonnaise, sour cream, green onions, pepper and Cajun seasoning in a bowl and mix well. Chill for 8 to 10 hours. Serve with corn chips.

Yield: 10 to 12 servings

Nancy Jackson, Product Sales Manager

Ro-Tel Dip

3 pounds Velveeta cheese, cut into 1-inch cubes
2 (10-ounce) cans Ro-Tel tomatoes with green chiles
1 pound ground chuck

Combine the Velveeta cheese and tomatoes in a microwave-safe dish. Microwave on High for 5 minutes or until the cheese is melted. Brown the ground chuck in a skillet, stirring until crumbly; drain. Add to the cheese mixture. Serve hot with corn chips.

Yield: 20 to 25 servings

Anna Irwin, Troop #275

Sausage Ro-Tel Dip

1 pound bulk pork sausage
2 pounds Velveeta cheese, cut into 1-inch cubes
2 (10-ounce) cans Ro-Tel tomatoes with green chiles

Brown the sausage in a large skillet until crumbly; drain. Combine with the Velveeta cheese and tomatoes in the top of a double boiler. Cook over medium-low heat until the cheese is melted and smooth, stirring occasionally. Serve with corn chips or tortilla chips.

Yield: 15 to 20 servings

Note: To prepare this dip in the microwave, combine 3 pounds Velveeta cheese cubes and 1/4 cup milk in a microwave-safe dish. Microwave on High for 5 minutes or until the cheese is melted. Add the browned sausage and tomatoes and mix well.

Danisha Williams, Troop #252

Hot Sausage and Cheese Dip

1 pound hot bulk pork sausage
1 pound ground beef
1 large onion, chopped
Salt and pepper to taste
1 (10-ounce) can cream of mushroom soup
2 pounds Velveeta cheese, cut into 1-inch cubes
1 (12-ounce) can evaporated milk
1 (8-ounce) jar picante sauce

Brown the sausage and ground beef with the onion in a skillet, stirring until the sausage and ground beef are crumbly; drain. Season with salt and pepper. Stir in the cream of mushroom soup.

Combine the Velveeta cheese, evaporated milk and picante sauce in a microwave-safe dish. Microwave on High for 5 minutes or until the cheese is melted. Combine the cheese mixture and the sausage mixture in a serving dish and mix well. Serve hot with corn chips.

Yield: 20 to 25 servings

Nancy Jackson, Product Sales Manager

Hot Chicken Dip

2 chicken breasts, cooked and chopped
1 (10-ounce) can cream of mushroom soup
1 (8-ounce) package cream cheese, chopped
1 (3-ounce) can mushroom pieces, undrained
1 (2-ounce) package slivered almonds
2 teaspoons dried parsley
1 teaspoon Worcestershire sauce
1/8 teaspoon garlic salt

Combine the chicken, cream of mushroom soup, cream cheese, mushroom pieces, almonds, parsley, Worcestershire sauce and garlic salt in a saucepan.

Cook over low heat until heated through. Remove to a serving dish and serve hot with large scoop-style corn chips.

Yield: 35 servings

Note: One 6-ounce can chicken, tuna or crab meat may be substituted for the chopped cooked chicken.

Council Recipe

Wild Duck Dip

2 wild ducks
1 slice bacon
1 medium onion, chopped
1 (8-ounce) can mushrooms or
  1 (8-ounce) package fresh mushrooms, sliced
6 tablespoons butter
1 (7-ounce) package wild rice,
  cooked using the package directions
2 teaspoons chopped fresh parsley
Butter
Salt and pepper to taste

Place the ducks in a roasting pan. Cover with the bacon slice.
Bake at 350 degrees for 4 to 5 hours or until tender. Remove the
breast and leg meat and chop finely in a food processor; discard
the skin and bones. Cook the onion and mushrooms in the butter
in a skillet until the onion is tender. Combine the mushroom
mixture, duck, wild rice and parsley in a large bowl. Add additional
butter to achieve desired consistency. Add salt and pepper to
taste. Remove the dip to a chafing dish and serve warm with
melba toast.

Yield: 10 to 12 servings

Sheila Chandler, Program Director

Crab Dip

1 (8-ounce) package Louis Kemp crab meat
1 (4-ounce) can deveined shrimp, drained
1 (8-ounce) package cream cheese, softened
2 tablespoons butter, softened
3 green onions, thinly sliced
1 tablespoon lemon juice
Worcestershire sauce to taste
Sour cream

Combine the crab meat, shrimp, cream cheese, butter and green onions in a bowl and mix well. Add the lemon juice, Worcestershire sauce and enough sour cream to make of spreading consistency. Serve with crackers.

Yield: 15 to 20 servings

Jeanne LeBlanc, Troop #39

Easy Shrimp Dip

1 (8-ounce) package cream cheese, softened
1 cup sour cream
2 teaspoons lemon juice
1 envelope Italian salad dressing mix
1 (4-ounce) can tiny shrimp, rinsed and drained

Combine the cream cheese, sour cream, lemon juice and salad dressing mix in a bowl and mix well. Stir in the shrimp.

Chill for 2$^{1}/_{2}$ to 3 hours. Serve with crackers or chips.

Yield: 10 to 12 servings

Council Recipe

Girl Scout Trivia
The Girl Scout motto is "Be Prepared."

Cheese Ball

2 (8-ounce) packages cream cheese, softened
1 (4-ounce) jar dried beef, finely chopped
1 bunch green onions, chopped
1 teaspoon MSG
1/4 cup chopped pecans

Combine the cream cheese, dried beef, green onions and MSG in a bowl and mix well. Shape into a ball. Roll the ball in the chopped pecans. Serve with crackers.

Yield: 10 to 12 servings

Peyten Eldridge, Carrollton Daisy Scouts Troop #373

Olive Cheese Ball

3 (8-ounce) packages cream cheese, softened
1 (2-ounce) jar dried beef, chopped
1 (4-ounce) can black olives, chopped
1 (3-ounce) can mushrooms, chopped
3/4 cup chopped celery
1 bunch green onions, chopped
1 tablespoon MSG
Chopped pecans

Combine the cream cheese, dried beef, black olives, mushrooms, celery, onions and MSG in a bowl and mix well. Shape into a ball. Roll the ball in the chopped pecans.

Yield: 20 to 25 servings

Nancy Jackson, Product Sales Manager

Cheddar Cheese Ball

2 (8-ounce) packages cream cheese, softened
8 ounces sharp Cheddar cheese, shredded
2 ounces blue cheese, crumbled
1 cup chopped black olives
1 teaspoon Worcestershire sauce
Dash of Tabasco sauce
1/4 cup chopped fresh parsley

Combine the cream cheese, Cheddar cheese, blue cheese, black olives, Worcestershire sauce and Tabasco sauce in a bowl and mix well.

Shape into a ball. Roll the ball in the chopped parsley.

Yield: 20 to 25 servings

Cindy Herring, Assistant Executive Director

Cheese Ring with Strawberry Preserves

4 cups (16 ounces) shredded Cheddar cheese
1 cup chopped pecans
3/4 cup mayonnaise
1/4 medium onion, finely chopped
1/2 teaspoon garlic salt
1/2 teaspoon Tabasco sauce
Lettuce leaves
Strawberry preserves, pepper jelly or chutney

Combine the cheese, pecans, mayonnaise, onion, garlic salt and Tabasco sauce in a bowl and mix well. Spoon into a greased bundt pan.

Chill for 24 hours. Unmold onto a lettuce-lined serving plate. Spoon strawberry preserves into the center of the ring.

Yield: 25 to 30 servings

Nancy Jackson, Product Sales Manager

Hot Artichoke Spread

**1 (14-ounce) can artichoke hearts,
    drained and finely chopped
1 cup mayonnaise
1 cup (4 ounces) grated Parmesan cheese
1 envelope Italian salad dressing mix**

Combine the artichoke hearts, mayonnaise, Parmesan cheese and salad dressing mix in a food processor and process until smooth. Pour into a greased baking dish.

Bake at 350 degrees for 20 minutes. Serve warm with crackers.

Yield: 25 servings

Council Recipe

Cheese Straws

1/2 cup (1 stick) butter or margarine, softened
1 (5-ounce) jar Old English cheese spread
11/2 cups sifted flour
1/2 teaspoon salt
1/2 teaspoon cayenne pepper

Cream the butter and cheese spread in a mixing bowl. Add the flour, salt and cayenne pepper and mix well. Place the dough in a cookie press. Press desired shapes onto a greased cookie sheet.
Bake at 375 degrees for 15 minutes.

Yield: 4 dozen

Nancy Jackson, Product Sales Manager

Cajun Trash

1/2 cup (1 stick) margarine
1 tablespoon parsley flakes
1 teaspoon celery salt
1 teaspoon garlic powder
1/2 teaspoon cayenne pepper
8 drops of Tabasco sauce
2 cups Wheat Chex
2 cup Corn Chex
2 cups Rice Chex
2 cups plain Cheerios
1 cup peanuts
1 (3-ounce) can French-fried onions

Melt the margarine in a baking pan in a 350-degree oven. Add the parsley flakes, celery salt, garlic powder, cayenne pepper and Tabasco sauce and mix well. Add the Chex cereals, Cheerios and peanuts and stir until well coated. Bake at 350 degrees for 20 to 25 minutes, stirring halfway through baking time. Stir in the French-fried onions. Spread on paper towels to cool. Store the mix in an airtight container.

Yield: 9 cups

Josephine Howard, Troop #97

Sausage-Stuffed Mushrooms

**24 fresh mushrooms (about 1 pound),
    rinsed and dried
1 pound bulk pork sausage
1 teaspoon minced garlic
2 tablespoons chopped parsley
1½ cups (6 ounces) shredded
    Cheddar cheese
1 (3-ounce) package cream cheese, chopped**

Remove the mushroom stems from the caps and chop the stems.
Brown the sausage with the mushroom stems, garlic and parsley
in a skillet, stirring until the sausage is crumbly; drain. Add the
Cheddar cheese and cream cheese and mix well.

Spoon into the mushroom caps. Arrange the caps in an
ungreased 9×13-inch baking dish. Bake at 350 degrees for
20 minutes.

Yield: 24 mushrooms

Sheila Chandler, Program Director

Snack Pizzas

1 (10-count) can flaky refrigerator biscuits
1 teaspoon oregano
1/4 cup tomato paste
1/4 cup chopped onion
1/3 cup canned mushrooms, chopped
1/2 cup (2 ounces) shredded sharp
    Cheddar cheese

Pat each biscuit into a 4-inch round on a greased baking sheet. Stir the oregano into the tomato paste. Spread on each biscuit round. Layer the onion, mushrooms and cheese over the tomato paste. Bake at 400 degrees for 8 minutes or until light brown.

Yield: 10 servings

Note: Other ingredients such as cooked ground beef or sausage, thin strips of salami, pepperoni, chopped green bell pepper or chopped anchovies may be used in place of the onion and mushrooms.

Norma Crowder, Troop #148

Swedish Meatballs

1 package fully cooked Italian meatballs
1 (16-ounce) can cranberry sauce
6 tablespoons steak sauce
4 teaspoons brown sugar
1 tablespoon vegetable oil
2 teaspoons prepared mustard

Combine the meatballs, cranberry sauce, steak sauce, brown sugar, oil and mustard in a slow cooker. Cook on High for 1 hour or until heated through.

Yield: 6 to 8 servings

Anna Irwin, Troop #275

Girl Scout Trivia
Girl Scouts of the U.S.A. provides international pen pals for girls ten to seventeen years old.

Chinese Chicken Wings

14 chicken wings (about 2 pounds)
1/3 cup tamari or soy sauce
1/3 cup pineapple juice
2 tablespoons water
1 tablespoon honey
1 tablespoon sunflower-seed oil
1 teaspoon minced garlic
1 teaspoon grated fresh gingerroot

Disjoint the chicken wings and discard the tips. Arrange in a baking pan. Combine the tamari, pineapple juice, water, honey, sunflower-seed oil, garlic and gingerroot in a small bowl and mix well. Pour over the chicken wings. Marinate, covered, in the refrigerator for 8 to 10 hours. Arrange the wings on a foil-lined baking sheet. Pour 1/2 cup of the marinade over the wings. Bake at 350 degrees for 30 to 40 minutes or until the chicken is cooked through.

Yield: 14 servings

Ayrianna Cooks, Troop #259

Grilled Dove Breast Appetizers

24 dove breasts
12 slices bacon, cut into halves
2 cups Worcestershire sauce
1 teaspoon garlic powder
Pepper to taste

Wrap each dove breast in 1bacon piece and secure with a wooden pick. Arrange in a shallow pan. Combine the Worcestershire sauce, garlic powder and pepper in a bowl and pour over the dove breasts. Marinate, covered, in the refrigerator for 2 hours.

Grill the dove breasts over hot coals for 15 minutes on each side or until cooked through, basting frequently with the marinade.

Yield: 24 servings

Sheila Chandler, Program Director

Party Ham Sandwiches

1 cup (2 sticks) margarine, melted
2 teaspoons Creole mustard
1/4 teaspoon grated onion
24 small sesame seed rolls, split
1 (12-ounce) package sliced ham
8 ounces Monterey Jack cheese,
  sliced or shredded

Combine the margarine, mustard and onion in a bowl and mix well. Spread the cut sides of the rolls with the margarine mixture. Place the ham and cheese on each roll bottom and replace the roll tops.

Bake the sandwiches, wrapped tightly in foil, at 350 degrees for 30 minutes.

Yield: 24 sandwiches

Council Recipe

Shrimp and Bacon Wraps

24 deveined peeled large fresh shrimp
3 tablespoons butter
Juice of 1/2 lime
12 slices bacon, cut into halves
1/2 cup barbecue sauce
1 cup (4 ounces) shredded
mozzarella cheese

Cook the shrimp in the butter and lime juice in a skillet for 2 minutes or until the shrimp are slightly undercooked, turning once; drain. Let stand until cool. Place the bacon slices in a microwave-safe dish lined with paper towels. Microwave on High for 1 minute. Let stand until cool. Wrap each shrimp in a bacon slice and arrange in a baking pan. Bake at 350 degrees for 5 minutes. Brush the shrimp with the barbecue sauce and sprinkle with the cheese. Broil 6 inches from the heat source for 2 minutes.

Yield: 24 servings

Querrida Johnson, Troop #162

Soups & Salads

Soup Tips

- ❖ Refrigerate cooked stews and soups overnight before serving. The fat will rise to the top and you can skim it off easily before heating and serving.

- ❖ In a hurry to skim the fat from soup? An ice cube floated in the soup will help to harden the fat and make it easier to remove.

- ❖ A leaf of lettuce dropped into a pot of soup will absorb fat on the surface.

- ❖ Soups and stews should only simmer, NEVER BOIL, when cooking.

- ❖ Freeze the liquid from canned mushrooms or vegetables; use it to enrich your soups or stews.

Salad Tips

A good salad is a mixture of different textures and flavors. Instead of just plain iceberg lettuce, mix a soft butter lettuce with a crisp, mild-flavored romaine or a stronger-flavored leaf lettuce. A few leaves of radicchio, arugula, watercress or baby organic greens will make your salad even more interesting.

After bringing your greens home, wash them in cold water and spin them dry. Besides diluting your dressing, excess moisture will spoil the greens more quickly. Store the washed greens in sealable plastic bags or plastic containers with a slightly damp paper towel at the bottom to maintain humidity.

Beef and Vegetable Soup

2 oxtails
4 or 5 ribs celery, chopped
4 or 5 carrots, sliced
1 large onion, chopped
2 teaspoons minced garlic
2 (10-ounce) cans beef
 broth
Freshly ground pepper
8 bay leaves
1 pound stew beef, cut into
 small pieces
1 (26-ounce) can tomato
 soup
1 quart water

1 (12-ounce) can tomato
 paste
2 vegetable bouillon cubes
1 (15-ounce) can black-
 eyed peas
8 ounces frozen cut okra
8 ounces frozen green peas
8 ounces frozen butter peas
8 ounces frozen green beans
16 ounces frozen Shoe Peg
 corn
1/2 small cabbage, chopped
8 ounces macaroni
Salt to taste

Combine the oxtails, celery, carrot, onion and garlic in a roasting pan. Roast at 375 degrees until golden brown. Remove to a slow cooker. Add the beef broth and enough water to fill the slow cooker 3/4 full. Add the pepper and bay leaves. Cook on Low for 10 hours. Remove the oxtails and the bay leaves. Brown the stew beef in a large Dutch oven. Add the oxtail broth and vegetables from the slow cooker, tomato soup, water, tomato paste, bouillon cubes, black-eyed peas, okra, green peas, butter peas, green beans, corn and cabbage. Bring to a boil. Reduce the heat and simmer until the beef is tender, stirring frequently. Add the macaroni. Cook for 10 minutes or until the macaroni is tender. Add salt and more water to thin to desired consistency.

Yield: 16 to 20 servings

Josephine Howard, Troop #97

Chili

2 pounds ground chuck
2 medium onions, chopped
1 garlic clove, pressed
Vegetable oil
3 (10-ounce) cans tomato soup
3 soup cans water
2 tablespoons chili powder
1 tablespoon cumin
1 teaspoon oregano
1 1/2 teaspoons salt
1/2 to 1 teaspoon red pepper
2 (20-ounce) cans kidney beans,
    drained and rinsed

Brown the ground chuck with the onions and garlic in a small amount of oil in a skillet until the ground chuck is crumbly; drain. Add the tomato soup, water, chili powder, cumin, oregano, salt and pepper and mix well. Bring to a boil. Reduce the heat and simmer for 45 to 60 minutes. Add the kidney beans. Simmer for 1 hour longer.

Yield: 6 to 8 servings

Brooke Canterbury, Troop #97

Italian Chicken Soup

1 chicken, skin removed
1 small package chicken thighs, skin removed
3 pounds onions, chopped
1 rib celery, chopped
1 (28-ounce) can tomatoes, chopped
1 (16-ounce) can tomatoes, chopped
Salt and pepper to taste
1¹/₂ cups (6 ounces) grated Romano cheese
1 (16-ounce) package angel hair pasta,
**   broken into small pieces**

Combine the whole chicken, chicken thighs, onions, celery and tomatoes in a 12-quart stockpot. Fill the pot with water. Add salt and pepper. Bring to a boil. Reduce the heat and simmer for 1¹/₂ hours or until the chicken falls from the bone. Remove the chicken from the broth. Let stand until cool. Chop the chicken, discarding the bones. Add the angel hair pasta to the broth. Cook until tender. Add the chopped chicken to the broth. Stir in the cheese. Adjust the seasonings.

Yield: 20 to 25 servings

August Malouf, Troop #97

Pumpkin Soup

2 cups chicken broth
4 cups canned pumpkin
2 to 3 cups milk, scalded
3 tablespoons butter
3 tablespoons brown sugar
1 cup finely chopped ham
Nutmeg to taste
Salt and pepper to taste

Whisk the chicken broth into the pumpkin in a large saucepan. Stir in enough of the milk to reach desired consistency. Add the butter, brown sugar, ham, nutmeg, salt and pepper. Heat to just below the boiling point. Ladle the soup into bowls and garnish with additional nutmeg.

Yield: 4 to 6 servings

Note: A large slow cooker set on Low works very well for this dish.

Querrida Johnson, Troop #162

Taco Soup

1 pound ground beef
1/2 medium onion, chopped
1 (15-ounce) can whole kernel corn
1 (20-ounce) can kidney beans
1 (14-ounce) can diced stewed tomatoes
1 envelope taco seasoning mix
11/2 teaspoons chili powder
1/2 teaspoon garlic powder

Brown the ground beef with the onion in a Dutch oven, stirring until the ground beef is crumbly; drain. Add the corn, kidney beans, tomatoes, taco seasoning mix, chili powder and garlic powder and mix well. Bring to a boil. Reduce the heat and simmer, covered, for 15 minutes. Serve the soup with sour cream, shredded cheese and crushed tostadas or corn chips.

Yield: 6 to 8 servings

Note: This soup freezes well.

Josephine Howard, Troop #97

Tortellini Soup

4 garlic cloves
1 tablespoon butter
3 1/2 cups chicken stock
1 (9-ounce) package cheese tortellini
1/4 cup (1 ounce) grated Parmesan cheese
Salt and pepper to taste
1 (14-ounce) can stewed tomatoes
1/2 bunch spinach, stems removed
6 fresh basil leaves, or 1/2 teaspoon dried basil

Cook the garlic in the butter in a large soup pot for 2 minutes. Stir in the chicken stock and tortellini. Bring to a boil. Reduce the heat and add the cheese, salt and pepper. Simmer for 5 minutes or just until the tortellini are tender. Stir in the tomatoes, spinach and basil. Simmer for 2 minutes longer. Serve with additional Parmesan cheese.

Yield: 4 servings

Sue Serratt, Field Executive

Girl Scout Trivia
Juliette Gordon Low, founder of the Girl Scouts in the U.S.A., has been recognized for her achievements in many ways. There is a commemorative stamp, a liberty ship, and a new federal building named for her.

White Bean Chili

1 onion, chopped
1 tablespoon olive oil
2 garlic cloves, minced
4 boneless skinless chicken breasts, chopped
3 cups water
2 teaspoons cumin
1 teaspoon chili powder
1 teaspoon oregano
1 teaspoon salt
1 teaspoon pepper
2 (15-ounce) cans Great Northern beans, drained
1 (14-ounce) can chicken broth
2 (15-ounce) cans Great Northern beans, drained
1 (16-ounce) package frozen Shoe Peg corn
2 (4-ounce) cans chopped green chiles
3 tablespoons lime juice

Cook the onion in the olive oil in a large Dutch oven over medium-high heat for 7 minutes. Add the garlic and cook for 2 to 3 minutes. Stir in the chicken. Cook until the chicken is light brown, stirring constantly. Add the water, cumin, chili powder, oregano, salt and pepper. Bring to a boil. Reduce the heat and simmer for 10 minutes or until the chicken is tender and cooked through, stirring frequently. Process 2 cans of the beans and the chicken broth in a blender until smooth. Add the bean purée, remaining 2 cans beans, corn and green chiles to the Dutch oven. Bring to a boil. Reduce the heat and simmer for 30 minutes, stirring frequently. Stir in the lime juice just before serving.

Yield: 16 servings

Josephine Howard, Troop #97

Seafood Gumbo

6 tablespoons flour
1/2 cup olive oil
11/2 cups chopped onions
1/2 cup chopped celery
1/2 cup chopped green
   bell pepper
1 (10-ounce) package
   frozen okra
1 (16-ounce) can tomatoes,
   chopped
21/2 quarts water
2 tablespoons chopped
   fresh parsley
2 teaspoons minced garlic

2 teaspoons Tabasco sauce
1 tablespoon Southern
   Cajun Seasoning
   (page 77)
1 teaspoon ground
   bay leaves
1/2 teaspoon thyme
2 pints oysters with their
   liquor
2 to 3 pounds peeled
   shrimp
1 pound crab meat, flaked
Hot cooked rice

Brown the flour slowly in the olive oil in a large soup pot, stirring constantly to make a roux. Add the onions, celery and bell pepper and cook until the vegetables soften. Add the okra, tomatoes, water, parsley, garlic, Tabasco sauce, Southern Cajun Seasoning, bay leaves, thyme and the liquor from the oysters. Bring to a boil. Lower the heat and simmer for 1 hour. Add the oysters, shrimp and crab meat. Cook for 15 to 20 minutes longer. Remove the bay leaves, if possible. Serve the gumbo over fluffy rice.

Yield: 10 to 14 servings

Brittany Roby, Cadette

Southern Cajun Seasoning

1 (26-ounce) box salt (or light salt)
1/4 cup cayenne pepper
3 tablespoons black pepper
2 tablespoons garlic powder
2 tablespoons chili powder
2 tablespoons dried parsley
2 tablespoons MSG (optional)
1 teaspoon onion powder
1 teaspoon nutmeg

Combine the salt, cayenne pepper, black pepper, garlic powder, chili powder, dried parsley, MSG, onion powder and nutmeg in a large bowl and mix well. Fill a shaker with the seasoning for daily use. Store the remainder in an airtight container.

Yield: about 31/2 cups

Brittany Roby, Cadette

Ambrosia Salad

5 oranges, peeled and sliced
4 bananas, sliced
2 (16-ounce) packages frozen strawberries
1 (20-ounce) can pineapple chunks
1 quart shredded or flaked coconut
1/2 cup sugar
1 cup cooking sherry
Whole strawberries

Combine the oranges, bananas, strawberries and pineapple chunks in a bowl. Drain off the juices and reserve. Sprinkle the bottom of a serving bowl with 1/3 of the coconut. Layer 1/2 of the fruit and sugar over the coconut. Repeat the layers. Sprinkle with remaining 1/3 of the coconut.

Combine the reserved juices and the sherry. Pour over the fruit. Top with whole strawberries. Chill until serving time (the longer the better).

Yield: 7 to 8 servings

Jasmaine Willis, Troop #122

Cherry Coke Salad

1 (15-ounce) can pineapple tidbits
1 (15-ounce) can Bing cherries
2 (3-ounce) packages cherry-flavored gelatin
2 (12-ounce) cans Coca-Cola
1 (8-ounce) package cream cheese, chopped
1 cup chopped nuts

Drain the pineapple and cherries, reserving the juices. Dissolve the gelatin in the fruit juices in a bowl. Add the Coca-Cola, pineapple, cherries, cream cheese and nuts and mix well. Chill until firm.

Yield: 6 to 8 servings

Kiyona Crawford, Troop #122

Frozen Orange Salad

1 (3-ounce) package orange-flavored gelatin
1 cup hot water
1 quart pineapple sherbet
1 (11-ounce) can mandarin oranges, drained
1 quart whipped topping

Dissolve the gelatin in the hot water in a bowl. Chill until partially set. Add the sherbet, mandarin oranges and whipped topping and mix well. Freeze until firm.

Yield: 6 to 8 servings

Nancy Jackson, Product Sales Manager

Broccoli Salad

1 large bunch broccoli crowns, chopped
1 medium red onion, minced
1 to 1 1/2 cups golden raisins
1/2 (4-ounce) jar bacon bits
1 cup mayonnaise
1/2 cup sugar
3 tablespoons tarragon vinegar

Combine the broccoli, onion, raisins and bacon bits in a bowl. Combine the mayonnaise, sugar and vinegar in a small mixing bowl and beat well. Pour over the broccoli mixture and stir to coat. Marinate in the refrigerator for several hours before serving.

Yield: 4 to 6 servings

Note: Make this a wonderful low-cholesterol salad by using a light mayonnaise and cholesterol-free bacon bits.

Sherry Kelly, Communications Director

Easy Garden Corn Salad

   3 tablespoons olive oil
   3 tablespoons cider vinegar
   1 (11-ounce) can mixed yellow and
       white niblet corn
   1 large tomato, seeded and
       cut into 1/2-inch pieces
   1 cup (4 ounces) shredded mozzarella cheese
   1/4 cup chopped fresh basil, or
       2 teaspoons dried basil

Whisk the olive oil and cider vinegar together in a salad bowl. Add the corn, tomato, cheese and basil and toss to mix. Chill thoroughly before serving.

Yield: 4 servings

Anne Kristen Wigington, Troop #39

Shoe Peg Corn Salad

2 (11-ounce) cans Shoe Peg corn, drained
6 tomatoes, cut into small cubes
3 green onions, chopped
3 to 4 tablespoons mayonnaise

Combine the Shoe Peg corn, tomatoes, green onions and mayonnaise in a salad bowl and mix well. Chill thoroughly before serving.

Yield: 8 servings

Yumeka McCray, Troop #122

Kansas Cucumber Salad

1 cup mayonnaise
1/2 cup sugar
4 teaspoons vinegar
1/2 teaspoon dill weed
1/2 teaspoon salt (optional)
4 medium cucumbers, peeled and thinly sliced
3 green onions (optional)

Combine the mayonnaise, sugar, vinegar, dill weed and salt in a salad bowl and mix well. Add the cucumbers and green onions and mix well.

Chill, covered, for 1 hour or longer.

Yield: 8 servings

Julianne Linder, Troop #83

Seven-Layer Salad

1 head lettuce, chopped
3 small tomatoes, cut into small cubes
2 green bell peppers, cut into 1/2-inch pieces
2 cucumbers, thinly sliced
1 bunch green onions, thinly sliced
1 large red onion, cut into strips
1 (10-ounce) package frozen green
**   peas**
1 cup mayonnaise-type salad dressing

Layer the lettuce, tomatoes, bell peppers, cucumbers, green onions, red onion and still-frozen peas in a large salad bowl. Spread the salad dressing over the top layer, sealing to the edge. Chill thoroughly before serving.

Yield: 4 servings

Note: My Aunt Leola Hill showed me how to make this salad.

Nahdra Curry, Troop #88

Macaroni Salad

1 (7-ounce) package macaroni and
    cheese dinner
1 cup chopped celery
1/2 cup chopped green bell pepper
1 (4-ounce) jar pimentos, drained and chopped
1/2 cup mayonnaise
1 tablespoon vinegar
Salt and pepper to taste

Cook the macaroni and cheese dinner using the package directions. Spoon the macaroni and cheese into a salad bowl. Add the celery, bell pepper, pimentos, mayonnaise, vinegar, salt and pepper and mix well. Chill thoroughly before serving.

Yield: 6 to 8 servings

Troop #88

Baked Potato Salad

10 ounces cream cheese, softened
2 cups sour cream
1 1/2 cups mayonnaise
1 1/2 pounds bacon, crisp-cooked and crumbled
1/3 cup chopped green onions
1/2 cup creamy Italian salad dressing
Dash of Worcestershire sauce
1 teaspoon garlic powder
1 teaspoon pepper
1/2 teaspoon salt
6 large baking potatoes, baked, cooled
**   and cut into 1/2-inch pieces**

Combine the cream cheese and sour cream in a large salad bowl and mix well. Add the mayonnaise, bacon, green onions, Italian salad dressing, Worcestershire sauce, garlic powder, pepper and salt and mix well. Stir the potatoes into the mayonnaise mixture.

Yield: 8 to 10 servings

Sue Seratt, Field Executive

Chicken Salad

1 1/2 cups chopped cooked chicken
1 cup chopped celery
2/3 cup seedless white grapes, halved
1/4 cup mayonnaise
Lettuce leaves

Combine the chicken, celery, grapes and mayonnaise in a bowl
and mix well. Chill thoroughly and serve on crisp lettuce leaves.

Yield: 4 or 5 servings

Deshundria Mitchell, Troop #122

Chutney Chicken Salad

1 cup mayonnaise
1/2 cup chutney
8 chicken breasts, cooked and chopped
2 ribs celery, coarsely chopped
4 green onions, coarsely chopped
1 unpeeled Granny Smith apple, coarsely chopped,
    sprinkled with lemon juice
1/2 cup seedless red grapes, sliced
1/2 cup pecans, toasted
2 cups cooked brown rice

Whisk the mayonnaise and chutney together in a large serving
bowl. Add the remaining ingredients and mix well. Chill thoroughly.

Yield: 6 servings

Sue Seratt, Field Executive

Taco Salad

1 pound ground chuck
1 envelope taco seasoning mix
1 (6-ounce) can tomato paste
1 bag corn chips, crushed
1/2 head lettuce, chopped
1 tomato, chopped
1 (5-ounce) can black olives, sliced
2 cups (8 ounces) shredded cheese

Brown the ground chuck in a skillet, stirring until crumbly; drain. Add the taco seasoning mix, tomato paste and enough water to make the consistency of spaghetti sauce. Spread the crushed chips in a 9×13-inch baking pan. Layer the meat sauce, lettuce, tomato, black olives and cheese over the chips. Bake at 350 degrees until the cheese melts. Serve with your favorite salsa.

Yield: 8 to 10 servings

Jeanne LeBlanc, Troop #39

Shrimp Salad

1 pound cooked shrimp, peeled
1 cup sliced fresh mushrooms
1 cup sliced celery
1 (14-ounce) can bean sprouts
1/4 cup chopped green onions
1/2 cup lemon juice
Mayonnaise or mayonnaise-type salad dressing
Horseradish sauce to taste
Garlic salt to taste

Combine the shrimp, mushrooms, celery, bean sprouts, green onions and lemon juice in a salad bowl. Add the mayonnaise, horseradish sauce and garlic salt and mix well.

Chill thoroughly before serving.

Yield: 6 servings

Antwonette Keys, Troop #29

Salad Dressing

> **1 cup mayonnaise**
> **1 cup vegetable oil**
> **1 onion, grated**
> **1/4 cup ketchup**
> **2 garlic cloves, chopped**
> **2 tablespoons cold water**
> **1 teaspoon each horseradish, Worcestershire sauce,**
>   **prepared mustard, Tabasco sauce and paprika**

Combine the mayonnaise, oil, onion, ketchup, garlic, water, horseradish, Worcestershire sauce, mustard, Tabasco sauce and paprika in a jar with a tight-fitting lid. Shake well.

Yield: 2 1/2 cups dressing

Janet Young, Troop #7

Garlic Vinaigrette

> **3 garlic cloves, crushed**
> **Salt**
> **1/2 cup each vinegar, lemon juice and vegetable oil**

Combine the garlic and enough salt to make a thick paste in a small bowl. Add the vinegar, lemon juice and oil and blend with a fork. Chill until serving time.

Yield: 1 1/2 cups dressing

Cindy Herring, Assistant Executive Director

Italian Blue Cheese Salad Dressing

3/4 cup vegetable oil
1/4 cup olive oil
3 tablespoons balsamic vinegar
1 tablespoon white balsamic vinegar
2 to 3 tablespoons crumbled blue cheese
3 garlic cloves, crushed
1 teaspoon dry mustard
1 teaspoon salt
1 to 2 teaspoons freshly ground pepper

Combine the vegetable oil, olive oil, balsamic vinegar, white balsamic vinegar, blue cheese, garlic, mustard, salt and pepper in a bowl and whisk well. Serve on lettuce and spinach salads. Garnish with mandarin oranges and toasted pecans.

Yield: 1 1/4 cups dressing

Josephine Howard, Troop #97

Girl Scout Trivia
There are four World Centers where Girl Scouts and Girl Guides from all over the globe meet: Our Cabana in Mexico, Our Chalet in Switzerland, Pax Lodge in England, and Sangam in India.

Breakfast & Breads

Tips on Baking Bread

Yeast will last longer than the specified date printed on the packet if kept in the refrigerator, or even longer in the freezer, for up to a year. If you bake often, it is wise to purchase larger amounts of yeast and store it in the freezer. Place in a sealable plastic bag or glass container and mark the date of purchase. Bring the yeast to room temperature before using.

There is no law that says biscuits have to be round. Roll the dough into a rectangle and cut out square shapes. This way you won't have to reroll the dough.

Use nonstick cooking spray to grease the inside of the bowl in which you will be placing your yeast dough for rising. Spritz the top of the dough with the spray as well; this is a much neater method than trying to spread oil over the dough.

If you are interrupted in the midst of bread-rising, set the dough in the refrigerator. A long, cool rise will develop both texture and flavor.

Breakfast Casserole

1 pound bulk sausage
1/4 cup (1/2 stick) margarine, melted
6 slices white bread, crusts removed,
    torn into bite-size pieces
2 cups half-and-half
5 eggs, beaten
1 teaspoon salt
1 1/2 cups (6 ounces) shredded Cheddar cheese

Brown the sausage in a skillet, stirring until crumbly; drain. Spread the margarine in the bottom of a 9×13-inch baking dish. Layer the bread, half-and-half, eggs, salt, sausage and cheese over the margarine. Chill, covered, for 8 to 10 hours. Bake at 350 degrees for 40 to 50 minutes.

Yield: 6 to 8 servings

Sherry Kelly, Communications Director

The Best Quiche Lorraine

1 small bunch green onions, chopped
11/2 tablespoons butter
6 slices bacon, crisp-cooked and crumbled
6 thin slices ham, diced or shredded
1 (8-ounce) can mushrooms, drained
2 unbaked (9-inch) pie shells
1/2 to 3/4 cup (2 to 3 ounces) shredded Swiss cheese
6 eggs
11/2 cups evaporated milk
1 garlic clove, minced
1/2 teaspoon salt
1/2 teaspoon dry mustard
Dash of nutmeg
Dash of pepper

Cook the green onions in the butter in a skillet for 1 minute.
Spread the onion, bacon, ham and mushrooms in the pie shells.
Top with the cheese. Combine the eggs, milk, garlic, salt, mustard,
nutmeg and pepper in a small bowl and mix well. Pour over the
filled pie shells. Bake at 350 degrees for 35 minutes or until a knife
inserted near the center comes out clean.

Cover the pies with foil during baking if the edges are
browning too quickly.

Yield: 8 to 10 servings

Taylor Hays, Troop #270

Armadillo Eggs

1 pound hot bulk pork sausage
1 cup (4 ounces) shredded Cheddar cheese
2$1/2$ cups baking mix
4 ounces Monterey Jack cheese, sliced
6 to 8 jalapeño chiles, halved
1 egg, beaten
1 package Shake'n Bake for pork

Combine the sausage, cheese and baking mix in a large bowl and mix well. Shape into 1$1/2$-inch balls. Flatten each ball. Cover with a slice of cheese and a jalapeño chile half. Top with a little more of the sausage mixture.

Form each ball into the shape of an egg, completely enclosing the cheese and chile. Dip in the beaten egg and coat with the Shake'n Bake. Bake on an ungreased cooked sheet at 350 degrees for 40 minutes or until the sausage is cooked through.

Yield: 12 to 14 servings

Sherry Kelly, Communications Director

Biscuits

3 cups flour
1 teaspoon baking powder
1/2 cup (1 stick) butter
2 eggs

Combine the flour and baking powder in a bowl. Cut in the butter until crumbly. Add the eggs and stir with a fork until the mixture forms a ball. Pat 1/2 inch thick on a lightly floured surface. Cut with a biscuit cutter.

Place the biscuits on an ungreased baking sheet. Bake at 450 degrees for 10 minutes or until golden brown.

Yield: 10 to 12 biscuits

Ysonda Powell, Troop #128

Girl Scout Trivia
Girl Scouts and Girl Guides greet each other with a special handshake. A Girl Scout extends her left hand as a sign of friendship and loyalty while raising her right hand in the three-fingered Girl Scout sign.

Blueberry Streusel Coffee Cake

1 (2-layer) package yellow cake mix
1 (8-ounce) package cream cheese, softened
1/2 cup vegetable oil
1/2 cup sugar
1/4 cup milk
3 eggs
11/2 cups blueberries
Streusel Topping (below)

Combine the cake mix, cream cheese, oil, sugar, milk and eggs in a large mixing bowl. Beat until smooth. Pour into a greased 9×13-inch baking pan. Top with the blueberries. Drop the Streusel Topping by teaspoonfuls over the blueberries. Bake at 350 degrees for 45 to 50 minutes. Cool on a wire rack for 10 minutes. Cut into squares.

Yield: 12 servings

Streusel Topping

1/2 cup chopped pecans
1/4 cup packed light brown sugar
3 tablespoons melted butter
1/2 teaspoon cinnamon

Combine the pecans, brown sugar, butter and cinnamon in a small bowl and mix well.

Mary Kathryn Quigley, Troop #97

Banana Nut Muffins

2 cups flour
1/4 cup sugar
1 tablespoon baking powder
1/2 teaspoon salt
1 cup milk
1 egg, beaten
1/3 cup vegetable oil
3/4 cup mashed bananas
1/2 cup chopped walnuts

Sift the flour, sugar, baking powder and salt into a bowl and make a well in the center. Beat the milk with the egg, oil, bananas and walnuts in a mixing bowl. Pour into the well and stir just until moistened. Fill greased muffin cups 2/3 full. Bake at 400 degrees for 15 minutes or until golden brown or until a knife inserted near the center comes out clean.

Yield: 12 muffins

Alecia Williams, Troop #128

Blueberry Muffins

2 cups flour
1 teaspoon baking powder
1/4 teaspoon baking soda
1/2 teaspoon salt
1/2 cup (1 stick) butter or margarine, melted
1 cup sugar
2 eggs
1 cup sour cream
1 cup blueberries

Sift the flour, baking powder, baking soda and salt into a mixing bowl. Beat the butter, sugar, eggs and sour cream in a bowl. Add to the dry ingredients and stir just until moistened. Fold in the blueberries.

Fill greased muffin cups 2/3 full. Bake at 375 degrees for 25 minutes or until golden brown.

Yield: 12 muffins

Josephine Howard, Troop #97

Cornmeal Muffins

3/4 cup white cornmeal mix
1/4 cup flour
2 tablespoons sugar
1/2 cup milk
1 egg
3 tablespoons vegetable oil

Combine the cornmeal mix, flour and sugar in a mixing bowl. Beat the milk, egg and oil in a bowl. Add to the dry ingredients and stir just until moistened.

Fill paper-lined or greased muffin cups 2/3 full. Bake at 400 degrees for 18 to 22 minutes or until golden brown.

Yield: 6 muffins

Shertara Collins, Troop #29

Broccoli Corn Bread

2 (8-ounce) packages corn bread mix
4 eggs
1 cup (2 sticks) margarine, melted
1 cup chopped onion
**2 (10-ounce) packages chopped broccoli, partially
    cooked and drained**
8 ounces cottage cheese

Combine the corn bread mix, eggs, margarine, onion, broccoli
and cottage cheese in a bowl. Let stand for 5 minutes. Pour into
a greased 9×13-inch baking dish.

Bake at 425 degrees for 40 to 45 minutes or until golden
brown.

Yield: 10 to 12 servings

Josephine Howard, Troop #97

Fried Hot Water Corn Bread

4 cups water
2 cups cornmeal
3/4 teaspoon salt
1/2 teaspoon baking powder
Vegetable oil for frying

Bring the water to a boil in a saucepan. Combine the cornmeal, salt and baking powder in a heatproof bowl. Add 1/2 of the boiling water and mix well. Add more water to make a thick batter. Pat into round 1/2×3-inch portions. Deep-fry in hot oil until golden brown. Drain on paper towels.

Yield: 5 to 7 servings.

Note: This corn bread is great with homemade soup!

Sheila Chandler, Program Director

Buttermilk Hush Puppies

2 cups self-rising flour
2 cups self-rising cornmeal
1 teaspoon sugar
1/2 teaspoon salt
1/2 teaspoon pepper
1 large onion, grated
1 jalapeño chile, seeded and minced (optional)
2 cups buttermilk
1 egg
Vegetable oil for frying

Combine the flour, cornmeal, sugar, salt and pepper in a bowl. Stir in the onion and jalapeño chile. Beat the buttermilk and egg together in a bowl. Add to the flour mixture and mix well. Drop by level teaspoonfuls into 3 inches of 375-degree oil. Cook for 5 to 7 minutes or until golden brown. Drain on paper towels.

Yield: 5 dozen

Sheila Chandler, Program Director

Date Loaf

1 (8-ounce) package dates, chopped
2 tablespoons butter
1 teaspoon baking soda
1 cup hot water
1 egg
1 cup sugar
2 cups flour
1 1/2 cups nuts, chopped
1 teaspoon vanilla extract

Combine the dates, butter and baking soda in a small bowl. Add the hot water. Let stand until cool. Beat the egg and sugar in a mixing bowl. Add the date mixture and flour alternately, 1/2 at a time, mixing well after each addition. Stir in the nuts and vanilla.

Pour into a greased loaf pan. Bake at 325 degrees for 1 1/4 to 1 1/2 hours.

Yield: 1 loaf

Mary Alice Cates, Executive Director

Strawberry Bread

3 cups flour
2 cups sugar
1 teaspoon baking soda
1/2 teaspoon salt
1 tablespoon cinnamon
3 eggs, beaten
1 cup vegetable oil
2 (10-ounce) packages frozen sweetened sliced
strawberries, thawed

Combine the flour, sugar, baking soda, salt and cinnamon in a mixing bowl. Beat the eggs, oil and strawberries in a bowl. Add to the dry ingredients and mix well.

Pour into 2 greased and floured 5×9-inch loaf pans. Bake at 350 degrees for 1 hour.

Yield: 2 loaves

Cindy Herring, Assistant Executive Director

Monkey Bread

4 (10-count) cans buttermilk biscuits
1 cup sugar
1 tablespoon cinnamon
1/2 cup (1 stick) butter, melted

Cut each biscuit into quarters. Combine the sugar and cinnamon in a sealable plastic bag. Place 20 biscuit pieces in the bag at a time and shake well. Layer the biscuit pieces in a greased bundt pan.

Combine the butter and remaining cinnamon-sugar mixture and pour over the top of the biscuits. Bake at 350 degrees for 45 minutes. Invert onto a serving plate. Pull the bread apart into pieces to serve.

Yield: 10 to 12 servings

Victoria Marie Froid Bullard, Troop #115

Spoon Rolls

1 envelope dry yeast
4 cups self-rising flour
1/4 cup sugar
2 cups lukewarm water
3/4 cup melted shortening
1 egg
Dash of salt

Combine the yeast, flour and sugar in a bowl. Add the water, shortening, egg and salt and mix well.

Spoon into greased muffin cups. Bake at 425 degrees for 25 minutes.

Yield: 18 to 20 rolls

Janet Young, Troop #7

Note: It is not necessary for this dough to rise before baking.

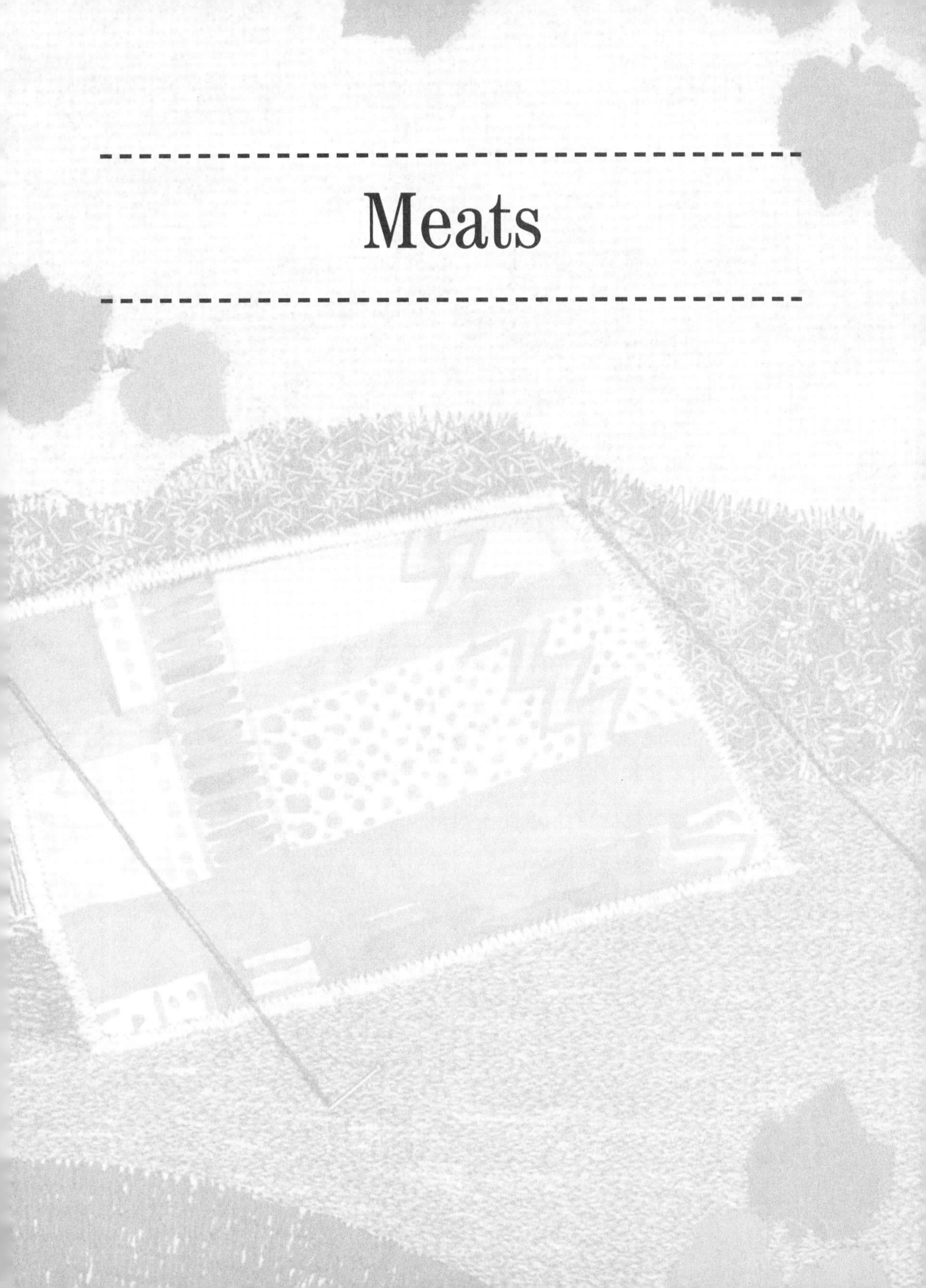

Meats

How To Season a New Cast-Iron Pot

A new cast-iron pot must be seasoned to ensure best results. The steps to follow are very simple:

1. Wash the pot thoroughly and wipe dry.

2. Place the empty pot on a stove-top burner and heat until extremely hot.

3. Carefully remove the pot from the burner and wipe the inside of the pot with a cloth saturated with shortening.

4. Place the pot back on the burner and heat until the bottom of the pot begins to smoke.

5. Remove the pot from the heat and wipe with a cloth saturated with vegetable oil, thoroughly coating the inside of the pot. Set aside and allow to cool.

6. After the pot cools to a temperature that allows handling, wipe any excess oil from the pot with a clean cloth.

Now you are ready to begin cooking.

Barbecued Brisket

1 (5- to 6-pound) beef brisket (flat cut)
3 ounces liquid smoke
Celery salt to taste
Garlic salt to taste
Onion salt to taste
Worcestershire sauce
Salt and pepper to taste
6 ounces barbecue sauce
2 tablespoons flour
1/2 cup water

Place the brisket in a large glass dish. Drizzle the liquid smoke over the brisket. Season with celery salt, garlic salt and onion salt. Marinate, covered, in the refrigerator for 8 to 10 hours. Place the brisket in a roasting pan; discard the marinade. Season with Worcestershire sauce, salt and pepper. Cover the pan loosely with foil. Bake at 275 degrees for 5 hours. Remove the foil. Pour the barbecue sauce over the brisket. Bake, uncovered, for 1 hour longer. Remove to a serving platter. Let cool before slicing. Skim the fat from the pan drippings and pour the drippings into a saucepan. Stir in the flour and water. Cook over medium heat until thickened, stirring constantly. Serve the hot sauce with the brisket.

Yield: 10 servings

Council Recipe

Grilled Boneless Top Round Roast

1 top round roast
Meat tenderizer
Garlic powder to taste
1 bottle Worcestershire sauce
1 bottle Italian salad dressing

Place the roast in a large glass dish. Sprinkle the meat tenderizer and garlic powder over both sides of the roast. Pour the Worcestershire sauce over the roast. Pierce the roast with a fork on both sides. Pour the Italian salad dressing over the roast.

Marinate, covered, in the refrigerator for 4 to 10 hours. Grill over hot coals for 10 to 12 minutes on each side.

Yield: 4 to 6 servings

Note: This recipe was served at a wedding party for us.

Anna Frances Morgan, Troop #97

Easy Chuck Roast

**1 (3- to 4-pound) boneless chuck roast,
    trimmed of fat
Greek seasoning to taste
Lemon pepper to taste
1 envelope onion-mushroom soup mix
1/2 cup water**

Place the roast in a slow cooker. Sprinkle with the Greek seasoning, lemon pepper and soup mix. Add the water.

Cook on Low for 8 to 10 hours. Thicken the drippings with flour or cornstarch, if desired.

Yield: 6 servings

Note: Any lean roast is good when cooked this way.

Council Recipe

Girl Scout Trivia
The founder of the Girl Scouts in the U.S.A. was born Juliette Kinzie Gordon. Her nickname was Daisy. Her married name was Juliette Gordon Low.

Easy Beef and Noodles

1 pound stew beef, cut into small pieces
1 (10-ounce) can cream of mushroom soup
1 envelope onion soup mix
1 cup red wine
Hot cooked egg noodles for 4 people

Combine the stew meat, cream of mushroom soup, soup mix and red wine in a bowl and mix well. Spoon into a casserole.

Bake, covered, at 300 degrees for 2¹/₂ hours. Serve over egg noodles.

Yield: 4 servings

Josephine Howard, Troop #97

Ground Beef Casserole

1¹/₂ pounds ground beef
¹/₂ cup chopped onion
¹/₂ cup chopped green bell pepper
1 egg, beaten
¹/₂ cup cooked rice
Salt to taste
1 envelope gravy mix
1¹/₂ cups water

Combine the ground beef, onion, bell pepper, egg, rice and salt in a bowl and mix well. Place in a casserole. Combine the gravy mix and water in a saucepan and mix well. Bring to a boil. Pour over the ground beef mixture. Bake at 350 degrees for 45 minutes or until the ground beef is cooked through.

Yield: 4 to 6 servings

Mary Alston, Leader, Troop #139

Johnny Marzetti

1½ pounds ground beef
1 pound onions, chopped
1 rib celery, chopped
Dash of Tabasco sauce
1 can tomato sauce
1 jar pasta sauce
1 (10-ounce) can tomato soup
1 (6-ounce) can tomato paste
2 cans mushroom pieces
1 bottle pimento-stuffed olives
8 ounces cheese, grated
½ green bell pepper, chopped (optional)
Dash of salt and pepper
2 packages wide egg noodles, cooked

Brown the ground beef with the onions and celery in a skillet, stirring until the ground beef is crumbly and the onions are translucent; drain. Combine the ground beef mixture, Tabasco sauce, tomato sauce, pasta sauce, tomato soup, tomato paste, mushroom pieces, olives, cheese, bell pepper, salt and pepper in a bowl and mix well. Stir in the noodles. Spoon into a large casserole. Bake, covered, at 300 degrees for 1 hour.

Yield: 12 servings

Note: This recipe is best if made a day in advance. It freezes well, too.

Nancy Jackson, Product Sales

Lasagna

1 large package lasagna noodles
1 tablespoon vegetable oil
1 pound ground beef
2 jars pasta sauce
2 cups cottage cheese
1 egg
1 cup (4 ounces) grated Parmesan cheese
1 package sliced mozzarella cheese
Grated Parmesan cheese
Shredded mozzarella cheese

Cook the lasagna noodles using the package directions, adding the oil if needed to prevent sticking. Brown the ground beef in a skillet, stirring until crumbly; drain. Stir in the pasta sauce. Combine the cottage cheese, egg and 1 cup Parmesan cheese in a bowl and mix well. Alternate layers of the noodles, cottage cheese mixture, ground beef mixture, sliced mozzarella cheese and additional Parmesan cheese in a greased casserole until all the ingredients are used. Top with shredded mozzarella cheese and additional Parmesan cheese. Bake, covered, at 350 degrees for 30 minutes. Uncover and bake for 15 minutes longer. Serve warm.

Yield: 6 to 8 servings

Derin Cook, Troop #39

Spaghetti Sauce

6 pounds ground round or ground chuck
6 pounds onions, chopped
2 ribs celery, chopped
3 tablespoons chopped garlic
1/3 bunch parsley, chopped
6 (6-ounce) cans tomato paste
2 gallons water
1 1/2 ounces dried mushrooms

Brown the ground round in a large Dutch oven or soup pot, stirring until crumbly; drain. Remove the ground round to a bowl.

Cook the onions, celery, garlic and parsley in the Dutch oven until brown, stirring frequently. Add the ground round, tomato paste, water and dried mushrooms and mix well. Bring to a boil. Reduce the heat and simmer for 3 to 4 hours.

Yield: 2 gallons sauce

Council Recipe

Pappa's Spaghetti Sauce

2¹/₂ pounds ground chuck
4 large onions, chopped in blender or
    food processor
1/2 (10-ounce) jar jalapeño chiles, chopped
    in blender or food processor
1 garlic clove, minced
1 (46-ounce) can tomato juice
Salt and pepper to taste

Brown the ground chuck in a Dutch oven, stirring until crumbly; drain. Add the onions, jalapeño chiles and garlic and mix well. Stir in the tomato juice.

Bring to a boil. Reduce the heat and simmer, covered, for 3 hours. Add the salt and pepper. Serve over spaghetti or thin spaghetti.

Yield: 6 to 8 servings

August Malouf, Troop #97

Western Mac

1 pound ground beef
1/2 cup sliced celery
1/4 cup chopped onion
1 (16-ounce) can whole kernel corn
1 (6-ounce) can tomato paste
6 cups water
1 package macaroni and cheese dinner
1 teaspoon salt
1/4 cup (1/2 stick) butter
1/4 cup 2% milk

Brown the ground beef in a skillet, stirring until crumbly; drain. Add the celery and onion. Cook until the vegetables are tender. Stir in the corn, tomato paste and 1/2 cup of the water.

Bring 6 cups of water to a boil in a saucepan. Add the macaroni and salt. Cook for 7 to 10 minutes or until tender; drain.

Combine the macaroni, butter, milk and contents of the sauce packet from the macaroni and cheese dinner in a bowl and mix well. Add the ground beef mixture and mix well.

Yield: 4 to 6 servings

Henrica William, Troop #29

Easy and Delicious Red Beans and Rice

**1 pound dried kidney beans,
     rinsed and sorted**
2 teaspoons salt
1 teaspoon pepper
1 bay leaf
1 teaspoon oregano
1 teaspoon paprika
Parsley
Tabasco sauce to taste
1 tablespoon Heinz 57 steak sauce
1 pound smoked sausage, sliced
Hot cooked rice

Combine the beans, salt, pepper, bay leaf, oregano, paprika, parsley, Tabasco sauce and steak sauce in a Dutch oven. Add water to 3 inches above the ingredients. Bring to a boil.

Cover the Dutch oven and turn off the heat. Let stand for 1 hour. Add the sausage. Bring to a boil.

Reduce the heat and simmer for 1 to 2 hours or until the sausage is cooked through. Mash some of the kidney beans to thicken the sauce; stir to mix again. Serve over the rice.

Yield: 6 to 8 servings

Josephine Howard, Troop #97

Stir-Fried Liver

**1 pound beef liver, thinly sliced
1 tablespoon cornstarch
1 garlic clove, crushed
2 tablespoons vegetable oil
1 onion, thinly sliced
5 mushrooms, sliced
3 scallions, chopped
1 teaspoon soy sauce**

Coat the liver with the cornstarch and garlic. Heat the oil in a skillet. Brown the liver in the hot oil. Add the onion and mushrooms. Stir-fry for 2 to 3 minutes. Add the scallions and soy sauce.

Cook for 6 to 9 minutes longer, stirring constantly.

Yield: 4 servings

Johnisha Brewer, Troop #122

Reuben Casserole

1/2 cup chopped onion
1 (16-ounce) can sauerkraut
1 cup sour cream
1 can corned beef, crumbled
**3 cups (12 ounces) shredded Swiss cheese or
    mozzarella cheese**
1/2 loaf rye bread, crumbled
1/2 cup (1 stick) margarine, melted

Combine the onion, sauerkraut and sour cream in a bowl and mix
well. Spread in a greased 9×13-inch baking dish.

Layer the corned beef, cheese and rye bread over the
sauerkraut mixture. Pour the margarine over the top. Bake at 350
degrees for 30 to 35 minutes.

Yield: 10 to 12 servings

Mary Alice Cates, Executive Director

Bacon-Stuffed Chicken Breasts

4 boneless skinless chicken breasts
3 slices bacon
1/4 cup chopped celery
1/4 cup chopped onion
2 cups seasoned stuffing mix for chicken
1/3 cup water
3 bacon slices, cut into halves
1 cup sour cream
1 tablespoon seasoned salt
2 teaspoons Worcestershire sauce
Dash of pepper

Pound the chicken 1/4 inch thick between sheets of waxed paper. Cook 3 slices bacon in a skillet until crisp; drain the bacon, reserving 3 tablespoons of the drippings in the skillet. Crumble the bacon. Add the celery and onion to the bacon drippings in the skillet. Cook until tender. Add the stuffing mix, water and crumbled bacon and mix well. Place 1/4 of the stuffing mixture on each chicken breast. Roll up to completely enclose the stuffing. Wrap each breast with 1/2 bacon slice. Place seam side down in a greased glass casserole. Bake at 350 degrees for 30 minutes. Combine the sour cream, seasoned salt, Worcestershire sauce and pepper in a bowl and mix well. Brush over the chicken. Bake for 30 minutes longer or until the chicken is cooked through.

Yield: 4 servings

Andie O'Bryant, Troop #8

Chicken and Dumplings

1 chicken, cut up
Salt to taste
1½ cups flour
1 tablespoon salt
¼ cup vegetable oil
⅓ cup ice water
¼ cup (½ stick) butter

Place the chicken in boiling salted water to cover in a large stockpot. Simmer until tender and cooked through. Remove the chicken, reserving the stock. Chop the chicken, discarding the skin and bones. Sift the flour and 1 tablespoon salt into a mixing bowl. Make a well in the center of the flour. Add the oil and water, stirring to make a stiff dough.

Return the chicken stock to a boil. Knead the dough lightly on a floured surface. Roll out very thin. Cut into blocks or strips and drop into the boiling chicken stock. Stir in the butter. Cook until the dumplings are tender. Add the chicken to the pot and heat through.

Yield: 10 servings

Brianna Thomas, Troop #122

Girl Scout Trivia
The Girl Scout emblem is fashioned in the shape of a three-leaf clover called a trefoil. The three leaves stand for the three parts of the Promise.

Chicken Barbecue Pizza

6 ounces boneless skinless chicken breast, chopped
1/2 cup chopped onion
1/2 cup barbecue sauce
6 cans crescent rolls
1/2 cup barbecue sauce
1/2 green bell pepper, chopped
1/2 red bell pepper, chopped
1/2 cup sliced mushrooms
1 small tomato, chopped
1 cup (4 ounces) shredded mozzarella cheese

Combine the chicken, onion and 1/2 cup barbecue sauce in a skillet. Cook until the chicken is cooked through. Press the rolls together to form a ball. Roll into a 13-inch circle on a lightly floured surface. Place on a 12-inch pizza pan coated with nonstick cooking spray.

Bake at 350 degrees for 10 minutes. Spread with 1/2 cup barbecue sauce. Top with the chicken mixture, bell peppers, mushrooms and tomatoes. Sprinkle with the cheese. Bake at 350 degrees for 10 to 15 minutes.

Yield: 2 to 4 servings

Gwen Guess, Troop #170

Chicken and Sour Cream Enchiladas

3 to 4 large chicken breasts, cooked and shredded
2 cups (8 ounces) shredded Monterey Jack cheese
2 cups (8 ounces) shredded longhorn cheese
1 (10-ounce) can cream of chicken soup
1 (4-ounce) can diced green chiles
2 cups sour cream
1 (4-ounce) can black olives, sliced
1 bunch green onions, whites and
   green tops chopped separately
12 flour tortillas

Combine the chicken, 1/2 of the Monterey Jack cheese, 1/2 of the longhorn cheese, the cream of chicken soup, green chiles, sour cream, olives and white parts of the green onions in a bowl and mix well. Spread a small amount in a greased 9×13-inch baking pan.

Fill the tortillas with the remainder of the chicken mixture. Roll up and arrange over the chicken mixture in the pan. Sprinkle with the remaining Monterey Jack cheese, longhorn cheese and green onion tops. Bake at 350 degrees for 30 minutes.

Yield: 8 to 12 servings

Kelsey Stephens, Troop #97

Fried Chicken

1 (3-pound) chicken, cut up
Seasoned salt to taste
Pepper to taste
Flour
Vegetable oil for frying

Rinse the chicken and pat dry. Season the chicken with seasoned salt and pepper. Coat with flour, shaking off any excess. Heat the oil in a skillet over medium heat. Cook the chicken in batches in the hot oil until golden brown and cooked through.

Yield: 4 servings

Cherrell Gallion, Troop #276

Fried Chicken Tenders

1 (12-ounce) can evaporated milk
2 eggs, beaten
2 to 3 tablespoons water
5 pounds chicken tenders or boneless
  skinless chicken breast strips
Garlic salt to taste
Pepper to taste
Flour
Vegetable oil for frying

Combine the milk, eggs and water in a shallow dish and mix well. Add the chicken. Marinate, covered, in the refrigerator for 8 to 10 hours.

Sprinkle the chicken with garlic salt and pepper. Coat with flour. Heat the oil in a skillet. Fry the chicken in the hot oil until golden brown and cooked through.

Yield: 10 servings

Jasmine Williams, Troop #122

Oven-Fried Chicken

2 cups sour cream
1/4 cup lemon juice
4 teaspoons Worcestershire sauce
4 teaspoons celery salt
2 teaspoons paprika
1 teaspoon garlic salt
1 teaspoon salt
1/2 teaspoon pepper
8 chicken breasts
2 cups cracker crumbs
1/2 cup (1 stick) margarine, melted

Combine the sour cream, lemon juice, Worcestershire sauce, celery salt, paprika, garlic salt, salt and pepper in a shallow dish. Add the chicken, turning to coat well. Chill, covered, for 8 to 10 hours. Coat the chicken with the cracker crumbs. Place in a shallow roasting pan. Pour 1/2 of the margarine over the chicken. Bake, uncovered, at 350 degrees for 45 to 60 minutes, basting occasionally. Pour the remainder of the margarine over the chicken. Bake for 15 minutes longer or until golden brown and cooked through. Cover the chicken with foil during the baking if it begins to brown too quickly.

Yield: 6 servings

Note: This recipe may be varied by coating the chicken with 1 cup Italian-style bread crumbs mixed with 1 cup grated Parmesan cheese and 1/4 cup chopped parsley.

Council Recipe

Chicken Tetrazzini

1¼ cups (5 ounces) shredded Cheddar cheese
2 tablespoons grated Parmesan cheese
2 cups chopped cooked chicken or turkey
1 (2-ounce) can diced pimento
¼ green bell pepper, cut into slivers
½ small onion, minced
1 (10-ounce) can cream of mushroom soup
½ cup chicken broth
Salt and pepper to taste
8 ounces spaghetti, broken into 2-inch pieces,
**   cooked and drained**
½ cup (2 ounces) shredded Cheddar cheese
2 tablespoons grated Parmesan cheese

Combine 1¼ cups Cheddar cheese, 2 tablespoons Parmesan cheese, chicken, pimento, bell pepper, onion, cream of mushroom soup, chicken broth, salt and pepper in a large bowl and mix well. Add the hot spaghetti and toss well.

Spoon into a greased casserole. Sprinkle with ½ cup Cheddar cheese and 2 tablespoons Parmesan cheese. Bake, covered, at 350 degrees for 45 minutes.

Yield: 6 to 8 servings

Council Recipe

Chicken Spaghetti

1 (3-pound) chicken or a hen
Salt to taste
12 ounces spaghetti
1 large onion, chopped
1 green bell pepper, chopped
1/2 cup (1 stick) margarine
1 can small green peas
1 (10-ounce) can tomatoes with green chiles, chopped
1 pound Velveeta cheese, cubed
1 cup milk
Garlic powder to taste
Pepper to taste

Place the chicken in boiling salted water to cover in a large pot. Simmer until tender and cooked through. Remove the chicken from the pot, reserving the broth. Chop the chicken, discarding the skin and bones. Cook the spaghetti in the reserved broth; drain. Cook the onion and bell pepper in the margarine in a skillet for 30 minutes or until tender. Add the spaghetti, peas, tomatoes with green chiles, Velveeta cheese and milk and mix well. Fold in the chicken. Season with garlic powder, salt and pepper. Spoon into a greased casserole. Bake at 350 degrees until bubbly.

Yield: 6 servings

Mattie L. Williams, Troop #122

Fast and Easy Jambalaya

1/2 teaspoon lemon pepper
1/2 teaspoon garlic powder
11/4 pounds boneless skinless chicken breast,
  cut into 1/2-inch pieces
Vegetable oil
12 ounces smoked Polish sausage,
  cut into 1/2-inch slices
1 medium onion, chopped
1 (16-ounce) jar picante sauce
1 (14-ounce) can Italian-style stewed tomatoes
1 can green peas
22/3 cups hot cooked rice

Sprinkle the lemon pepper and garlic powder over the chicken. Heat the oil in a skillet over medium-high heat. Cook the chicken in the hot oil until cooked through, stirring constantly. Add the sausage and onion. Cook for 5 minutes longer, stirring occasionally.

Stir in the picante sauce and tomatoes. Reduce the heat to medium. Cook for 12 minutes longer. Add the peas. Cook for 4 to 7 minutes longer or until the peas are tender. Serve over the rice.

Yield: 4 servings

Aberia Murphy, Troop #122

Hot Chicken Salad

2 cups chopped cooked chicken
2 cups diced celery
1 cup mayonnaise
1/2 cup grated onion
1/2 cup blanched almonds
2 tablespoons lemon juice
1/2 teaspoon salt
1/2 cup (2 ounces) shredded Cheddar cheese
2/3 cup crushed potato chips

Combine the chicken, celery, mayonnaise, onion, almonds, lemon juice and salt in a casserole coated with nonstick cooking spray. Top with the cheese and potato chips.

Bake at 375 degrees for 20 minutes or until bubbly and heated through.

Yield: 6 servings

Amy Bole, Troop #275

Russian Chicken

6 to 8 chicken breasts
4 chicken legs or thighs
1 (8-ounce) bottle Russian salad dressing
2 envelopes onion soup mix
1 (8- to 10-ounce) jar apricot preserves

Rinse the chicken and pat dry. Place the chicken in a large baking dish. Combine the salad dressing, soup mix and apricot preserves in a bowl and mix well. Pour over the chicken.

Bake, covered, at 300 degrees for 1 hour. Uncover and bake for 30 minutes longer or until the chicken is cooked through.

Yield: 6 servings

Anna Frances Morgan, Troop #97

Chicken and Asparagus Casserole

2 cups instant rice
2 cups boiling chicken broth
7 tablespoons margarine, melted
7 tablespoons flour
3 3/4 cups milk
1 1/2 teaspoons salt
1/2 teaspoon onion salt
12 slices American cheese
3 cups chopped cooked chicken
2 cans asparagus, drained

Combine the rice and chicken broth in a heatproof bowl and mix well. Cover and let stand until needed. Melt the margarine in a skillet over medium heat. Whisk in the flour. Cook for 2 minutes, stirring constantly.

Add the milk, salt and onion salt. Cook until thickened, stirring constantly. Layer 6 slices of the cheese, the chicken and asparagus over the rice. Pour the milk mixture over the layers. Top with the remaining 6 slices cheese. Bake at 350 degrees for 30 minutes or until bubbly.

Yield: 4 to 6 servings

Elizabeth Seratt, Junior Girl Scout

Sweet-and-Sour Chicken

4 boneless skinless chicken breasts
Salt and pepper to taste
2 tablespoons vegetable oil
1 onion, thinly sliced
2 medium carrots, julienned
1 (7-ounce) can pineapple chunks in its own juice
2 tablespoons wine vinegar
2 tablespoons brown sugar or honey
2 teaspoons tomato paste
1 tablespoon lemon juice
1/2 teaspoon Worcestershire sauce
1 red bell pepper, sliced
1 green bell pepper, sliced
2 teaspoons cornstarch

Season the chicken with salt and pepper. Heat the oil in a skillet. Cook the chicken in the hot oil until light brown. Remove to a greased casserole. Add the onion and carrots to the skillet. Cook for 2 to 3 minutes; drain. Drain the pineapple, reserving the juice. Add a mixture of the juice, vinegar, brown sugar, tomato paste, lemon juice and Worcestershire sauce to the skillet. Bring to a boil, stirring constantly. Stir in the pineapple. Layer the bell peppers over the chicken in the casserole. Pour the pineapple mixture over the peppers. Bake, covered with foil, at 375 degrees for 45 minutes or until the chicken and vegetables are tender and the chicken is cooked through. Remove the chicken to a serving dish. Pour the pan juices into a saucepan. Combine the cornstarch with a little cold water. Stir into the pan juices. Cook until thickened, stirring constantly. Pour over the chicken. Serve with boiled rice or jacket potatoes.

Yield: 4 servings

Kierra Dean, Troop #58

Chicken Ro-Tel

4 chicken breasts
1 package vermicelli
1/2 cup finely chopped onion
1/2 cup chopped green bell pepper
1 (10-ounce) can diced Ro-Tel tomatoes
1 pound Velveeta cheese, cubed
1 small can sliced mushrooms
1 small can tiny green peas
Shredded Cheddar cheese

Cook the chicken in boiling salted water to cover in a stockpot until tender and cooked through. Remove the chicken, reserving the broth. Chop the chicken and place in a greased casserole. Add the vermicelli to the reserved broth and cook until tender; drain. Add to the casserole.

Cook the onion and bell pepper in a skillet until tender. Add the tomatoes, Velveeta cheese and mushrooms, stirring until the cheese melts. Add the green peas. Spoon the vegetable mixture into the casserole, covering the vermicelli. Top with shredded Cheddar cheese. Bake at 350 degrees for 45 minutes.

Yield: 6 to 8 servings

Josephine Howard, Troop #97

Homemade Chicken Potpie

4 chicken breasts, cooked and chopped
4 hard-cooked eggs, sliced
1 (10-ounce) can cream of celery soup
1 (10-ounce) can chicken broth
1 (15-ounce) can mixed vegetables (optional)
1 cup self-rising flour
1 cup milk
1 cup (2 sticks) butter, melted
Pepper to taste

Place the chicken in a large greased casserole. Top with the sliced eggs. Combine the cream of celery soup, chicken broth and mixed vegetables in a bowl and mix well. Pour over the eggs.

Combine the flour, milk, butter and pepper in a bowl and mix well. Spoon over the casserole. Bake at 350 degrees for 1 hour or until the crust that forms is golden brown.

Yield: 4 to 6 servings

Katie Wilson, Troop #275

Turkey Dressing Casserole

2 cups chopped cooked turkey
2 cups (8 ounces) shredded American cheese
2 cups herb-seasoned stuffing mix
1 (10-ounce) can cream of mushroom soup
1 cup chopped celery
1 cup sour cream
1/2 cup milk
1/3 cup chopped onion
1/2 teaspoon rubbed sage
1/4 teaspoon pepper
1 cup herb-seasoned stuffing mix

Combine the turkey, cheese, 2 cups stuffing mix, the cream of mushroom soup, celery, sour cream, milk, onion, sage and pepper in a large bowl and mix well.

Pour into a greased 8×12-inch baking pan. Top with 1 cup stuffing mix. Bake at 350 degrees for 35 to 40 minutes or until bubbly.

Yield: 6 servings

Shaandrika Frierson, Troop #122

Pork Tenderloin Diane

1(1-pound) pork tenderloin, cut into 8 slices
2 teaspoons lemon pepper
2 tablespoons butter
1 tablespoon Worcestershire sauce
2 tablespoons lemon juice
1 teaspoon prepared mustard
Fresh minced parsley (optional)

Pound each tenderloin slice 1-inch thick. Sprinkle both sides with the lemon pepper. Heat the butter in a heavy skillet. Cook the tenderloin slices in the butter for 5 minutes on each side. Remove to a warm serving plate.

Add the Worcestershire sauce, lemon juice and mustard to the skillet. Cook until heated through, stirring constantly. Pour over the pork. Sprinkle with parsley.

Yield: 4 servings

Julianne Lindner, Troop #83

Marinated Pork Roast

**1 (4- to 5-pound) pork loin roast, boned,
   rolled and tied**
1/2 cup soy sauce
1/2 cup dry sherry
2 garlic cloves, minced
1 tablespoon dry mustard
1 teaspoon ginger
1 teaspoon thyme

Place the roast in a large sealable plastic bag. Combine the soy sauce, sherry, garlic, mustard, ginger and thyme in a bowl and mix well. Pour over the roast in the bag and seal tightly. Marinate in the refrigerator for 2 to 10 hours.

Remove the roast from the marinade, reserving the marinade. Place the roast on a rack in a roasting pan. Roast at 325 degrees for 3 hours or until a meat thermometer inserted into the thickest portion registers 175 degrees. Baste occasionally with the marinade during the last hour of roasting.

Yield: 8 to 10 servings

Wanda Perry, Council Receptionist

Fried Ribs

1 slab spareribs, cut into single ribs
Salt and pepper to taste
Vegetable oil
1 cup Italian salad dressing
Flour
Vegetable oil for frying

Season the ribs with the salt, pepper and vegetable oil. Place the ribs in a shallow dish. Pour the Italian salad dressing over the ribs. Let stand for 10 to 15 minutes.

Coat the ribs with flour. Heat the oil in a skillet. Fry the ribs in the hot oil until golden brown and cooked through.

Yield: 8 servings

Cynthia Thomas, Troop #122

Delta Blackened Catfish

2 teaspoons thyme
1 teaspoon cayenne pepper
1 teaspoon black pepper
1 teaspoon salt
3/4 teaspoon paprika
2/3 teaspoon garlic powder
1/2 cup (1 stick) butter, melted
Juice of 1 lemon
6 catfish fillets
1/4 cup dry white wine

Combine the thyme, cayenne pepper, black pepper, salt, paprika and garlic powder in a small bowl. Combine the butter and lemon juice in a shallow dish. Rinse the catfish fillets and pat dry. Dip the fillets in the butter mixture. Coat with the spice mixture.

Cook the fillets in a hot cast-iron skillet for 2 minutes on each side or until completely cooked. Remove the fillets to a warm serving plate. Pour the remaining butter mixture into the hot skillet quickly. Add the wine. Cook until hot, stirring constantly. Pour over the fillets.

Yield: 6 servings

Claudette Curry, Field Executive

Lemon Grilled Catfish

1/2 cup Worcestershire sauce
1/3 cup lemon juice
1/2 teaspoon cayenne pepper
4 drops of Tabasco sauce
1/2 teaspoon thyme
6 to 8 catfish fillets

Combine the Worcestershire sauce, lemon juice, cayenne pepper, Tabasco sauce and thyme in a large glass dish and mix well. Rinse the catfish fillets and pat dry. Place the fillets in the marinade. Marinate, covered, in the refrigerator for 1 to 4 hours. Remove the fillets from the marinade, reserving the marinade.

Grill the fillets over hot coals for 10 minutes, basting with the marinade and turning the fillets several times.

Yield: 6 servings

The Catfish Institute

Catfish Parmesan

1 egg, beaten
1 tablespoon milk
3/4 cup (3 ounces) grated Parmesan cheese
1/4 cup flour
1/4 teaspoon salt
1/2 teaspoon pepper
1 teaspoon paprika
6 catfish fillets
1/4 cup (1/2 stick) butter, melted
1/4 cup slivered almonds

Combine the egg and milk in a shallow dish. Combine the cheese, flour, salt, pepper and paprika on a plate. Rinse the catfish fillets and pat dry. Dip the fillets in the egg mixture. Coat with the cheese mixture.

Place the fillets in a single layer in a buttered baking pan. Chill until ready to cook. Drizzle the melted butter over the fillets. Top with the almonds.

Bake at 325 degrees for 40 minutes or until the fillets and almonds are crisp and golden brown.

Yield: 6 servings

Sesame Catfish

2 tablespoons sesame seeds
2 cups soft bread crumbs
1/2 teaspoon pepper
1/2 teaspoon thyme
1/3 cup melted butter
6 catfish fillets
1/2 teaspoon salt

Toast the sesame seeds in a dry skillet over medium heat for 3 to 4 minutes, shaking them frequently.

Combine the toasted sesame seeds, bread crumbs, pepper, thyme and butter in a shallow bowl and mix well. Rinse the catfish fillets and pat dry. Season the fillets with the salt.

Place the fillets in a single layer in a buttered baking dish. Spoon the bread crumb mixture over the fillets, pressing the crumbs into the fish. Bake at 350 degrees for 25 minutes or until the crumbs are golden brown.

Yield: 6 servings

Annie Roby, Field Executive

Southern Fried Catfish

6 catfish fillets
12 tablespoons (about) buttermilk
Salt and pepper to taste
White cornmeal
Peanut oil or other vegetable oil for frying

Rinse the catfish fillets and pat dry. Place the fillets in a shallow dish. Pour about 2 tablespoons buttermilk over each fillet, rubbing the buttermilk into the fish. Turn the fillets and coat the other side. Sprinkle lightly with salt and generously with pepper.

Coat the fillets with cornmeal in a bag or deep bowl. Heat the oil to 375 degrees in a skillet or deep fryer. Fry the fillets in the hot oil until light brown.

Yield: 4 servings

Kim O'Bryant, Camp Director

Mississippi Fried Oysters

Raw oysters, drained
2 eggs, beaten
2 cups cornmeal
2 tablespoons flour
1 teaspoon sugar
2 teaspoons salt
1 teaspoon pepper
Vegetable oil for frying

Combine the oysters and eggs in a bowl. Combine the cornmeal, flour, sugar, salt and pepper in a shallow dish.

Coat the oysters in the cornmeal mixture. Heat the oil in a deep fryer or skillet. Fry until golden brown. Drain on paper towels.

Servings: variable

Kim O'Bryant, Camp Director

Grilled Shrimp

2 pounds unpeeled large or jumbo shrimp
1 cup vegetable oil
1 cup lemon juice
2 teaspoons Italian salad dressing mix
2 teaspoons seasoned salt
1 teaspoon seasoned pepper
1 teaspoon Worcestershire sauce
1/4 cup packed brown sugar
2 tablespoons soy sauce
1/2 cup chopped green onions

Rinse the shrimp and drain on paper towels. Combine the oil, lemon juice, salad dressing mix, seasoned salt, seasoned pepper and Worcestershire sauce in a shallow bowl. Add the shrimp and mix well. Marinate in the refrigerator for 2 to 10 hours, stirring occasionally. Drain the shrimp, reserving the marinade. Thread the shrimp onto skewers. Grill over hot coals for 10 minutes, turning once and brushing with the marinade. Place the remaining marinade in a small saucepan. Add the brown sugar, soy sauce and green onions. Bring to a boil. Boil for 2 to 3 minutes, stirring constantly. Serve as a dip for the shrimp.

Yield: 8 servings

Kim O'Bryant, Camp Director

Shrimp Stroganoff

1 cup sour cream
1 (20-ounce) can cream of mushroom soup
1 teaspoon dill weed
1/4 cup sliced green onions
1/4 cup sliced black olives
1 (16-ounce) package frozen shrimp, thawed and
    drained
1 cup (4 ounces) shredded Cheddar cheese
1 (8-ounce) package medium egg noodles, cooked and
    drained

Combine the sour cream, cream of mushroom soup and dill weed in a large bowl and mix well. Add the green onions, olives, shrimp and 1/2 of the cheese and mix well. Stir in the noodles. Spoon into a lightly greased shallow 2-quart casserole.

Bake, covered, at 350 degrees for 30 minutes. Uncover and sprinkle with the remaining 1/2 cup cheese. Bake for 5 minutes longer or until the cheese melts.

Yield: 6 to 8 servings

Querrida Johnson, Troop #162

Impressive Shrimp

1 pound frozen cooked deveined shrimp
1/2 cup (1 stick) butter
1 cup Worcestershire sauce
1 tablespoon minced garlic

Thaw the shrimp in a bowl of cold water; drain. Melt the butter in a saucepan over low heat. Add the Worcestershire sauce and garlic. Bring to a boil, stirring constantly. Remove from the heat. Add the shrimp and mix well. Let stand for 10 minutes. Serve with a salad and garlic bread to dip in the sauce.

Yield: 4 to 6 servings

Note: To use fresh uncooked shrimp instead of the frozen, bake the shrimp in the marinade at 350 degrees for 10 to 15 minutes.

Janet Young, Leader, Troop #7

Potato Chip Casserole

1 (11-ounce) bag potato chips, crushed
1 (10-ounce) can cream of mushroom soup
1/2 cup milk
1 (6-ounce) can tuna, drained

Spread 1/2 of the potato chips in a greased casserole. Combine the cream of mushroom soup and milk in a bowl and mix well. Pour over the potato chips.

Layer the tuna and remaining potato chips over the soup mixture. Bake at 350 degrees for 25 minutes.

Yield: 4 servings

Dr. Mary Alice Cates, Executive Director of the Council

Delicious Tuna Noodle Casserole

1/2 large onion, chopped
2 ribs celery, chopped
Vegetable oil
8 ounces Velveeta cheese, cubed
1/2 cup cottage cheese
8 ounces macaroni, cooked
1 (12-ounce) can tuna
1 (10-ounce) package frozen green peas, thawed
2 to 4 dashes of red pepper

Sauté the onion and the celery in a little vegetable oil in a skillet until tender. Add the Velveeta cheese, cottage cheese, macaroni, tuna, green peas and red pepper. Stir until the cheese is melted and the macaroni is heated through.

Yield: 6 servings

Josephine Howard, Troop #97

Delta Frog Legs

1 (12-ounce) can evaporated milk
2 eggs, beaten
Salt and pepper to taste
10 pairs frog legs, split
Self-rising flour
Salt to taste
Vegetable oil for frying

Combine the evaporated milk, eggs, salt and pepper in a shallow bowl. Add the frog legs. Marinate, covered, in the refrigerator for 30 minutes or more. Remove the frog legs from the marinade, discarding the marinade.

Coat in self-rising flour seasoned with salt. Heat the oil to medium-hot in a skillet. Fry the frog legs in the oil until golden brown.

Yield: 4 to 6 servings

Sheila Chandler, Program Director

Duck Spaghetti

1 large wild duck
1 medium onion, chopped
1 tablespoon seasoned salt
2 tablespoons lemon pepper
1/2 cup diced pimentos
3/4 cup chopped green bell pepper
1 cup sliced canned mushrooms
1 (10-ounce) can cream of mushroom soup
1 (12-ounce) package spaghetti, cooked
2 cups (8 ounces) shredded Cheddar cheese

Cook the duck and onion in boiling water in a large stockpot until tender; drain, reserving the broth. Chop the duck, discarding the skin and bones. Season the duck meat with the seasoned salt and lemon pepper. Combine the duck, 1 cup of the reserved broth, the pimentos, bell pepper, mushrooms, cream of mushroom soup, spaghetti and 1 cup of the cheese in a bowl and mix well. Spoon into a greased 2-quart casserole. Top with the remaining 1 cup cheese. Bake at 350 degrees for 45 minutes.

Yield: 6 servings

Andie O'Bryant, Troop #8

Venison Steak Parmesan

4 tenderized boneless venison steaks, trimmed of fat
1 large egg, beaten
1 tablespoon water
1 teaspoon pepper
1 cup Italian-style bread crumbs
1/4 cup (1 ounce) grated Parmesan cheese
1/2 cup vegetable oil
1 cup pizza sauce or spaghetti sauce
1/4 cup (1 ounce) grated Parmesan cheese

Cut the steaks into strips or 4-inch squares. Combine the egg, water and pepper in a small bowl. Combine the bread crumbs and 1/4 cup Parmesan cheese in a dish.

Dip the steaks in the egg mixture. Coat with the bread crumb mixture. Brown the steaks in the oil in a large skillet over medium heat for 3 minutes on each side.

Arrange the steaks in an 8×8-inch baking dish. Top with the pizza sauce. Bake at 325 degrees for 20 minutes. Sprinkle with 1/4 cup cheese.

Yield: 4 servings

Andie O'Bryant, Troop #8

Venison Kabobs

1/2 venison backstrap
1 onion
2 tomatoes
1 green bell pepper
3 yellow squash
2 red potatoes
Soy sauce to taste
Worcestershire sauce to taste
Soul seasoning to taste

Cut the venison, onion, tomatoes, bell pepper, squash and potatoes into cubes. Thread the venison and vegetables alternately onto skewers.

Combine the soy sauce, Worcestershire sauce and soul seasoning in a shallow bowl. Add the kabobs. Marinate, covered, in the refrigerator for 2 hours. Grill over hot coals until cooked through.

Yield: 4 to 6 servings

Anna Irwin, Troop #275

Sauce for Wild Game

2 cups cider vinegar
Juice of 3 lemons
10 ounces Worcestershire sauce
5 ounces hot sauce
2 tablespoons soy sauce
2 tablespoons salt
4 tablespoons pepper
2 tablespoons sugar

Combine the vinegar, lemon juice, Worcestershire sauce, hot sauce, soy sauce, salt, pepper and sugar in a jar with a tight-fitting lid. Close the jar and shake well.

Store in the refrigerator. Use as a marinade on any wild game or meat.

Yield: 1 quart

Sheila Chandler, Program Director

Side Dishes

Buying Tips for Fruits and Vegetables

In general, never cut a fruit or vegetable until it is ready to eat. Another rule of thumb: never expect a fruit to ripen under refrigeration. Ripen first, then refrigerate.

Buy mature fruit. A green peach or nectarine, for example, will not ripen but merely soften and then wither. A cantaloupe picked too green will soften but will not be sweet and juicy. Some fruits do not gain sugar after harvest because they have no reserve starch for conversion to sugar. On the other hand, bananas and pears do gain sugar as well as tenderness after harvest.

Handle with care. Fresh fruits and vegetables require constant attention to keep their fresh appearance. The less you handle them, the longer their life. Don't pinch, squeeze, or poke them, for bruising leads to damage and damage results in more spoilage for you or your grocer.

Apple and Bean Pot

1 (53-ounce) can baked beans, well drained
1 large onion, chopped
3 tart apples, peeled and chopped
1/2 cup ketchup or barbecue sauce
1/2 cup packed brown sugar
1 package smoked cocktail sausages
**   (or use chopped hot dogs or cubes of ham)**

Place the beans in a slow cooker. Add the onion and apples and mix well. Stir in the ketchup, brown sugar and sausages.

Cook on Low for 3 to 4 hours. Increase heat to High. Cook for 30 minutes longer.

Yield: 10 to 12 servings

Sherry Kelly, Communications Director

Cranberry Casserole

1 pound fresh cranberries
3 cups chopped green apples
1/2 cup sugar
1/2 cup quick-cooking oats
1/2 cup packed brown sugar
1/2 cup chopped pecans
1/3 cup flour
1/2 cup (1 stick) butter, melted

Combine the cranberries, apples and sugar in a bowl and mix well. Spoon into a buttered 9×11-inch casserole.

Combine the oats, brown sugar, pecans and flour in a small bowl and mix well. Sprinkle over the cranberry mixture. Drizzle the melted butter over the top.

Bake at 350 degrees for 1 hour or until bubbly.

Yield: 8 servings

Sue Seratt, Field Executive

Pineapple Casserole

2 large cans pineapple chunks packed in juice
1/2 cup sugar
3 tablespoons flour
1 pound Velveeta cheese, shredded
1 sleeve butter crackers, crumbled
1/2 cup (1 stick) butter, melted

Drain the pineapple, reserving 6 tablespoons of the juice. Combine the sugar, flour and reserved pineapple juice in a small bowl and mix well.

Layer the pineapple chunks and Velveeta cheese in a buttered casserole. Pour the juice mixture over the layers. Sprinkle the crackers over the top. Drizzle with the butter.

Bake at 350 degrees for 30 to 40 minutes or until bubbly. Serve hot.

Yield: 4 to 6 servings

Anne Kristen Wigington, Troop #39

Asparagus Casserole

1 (13-ounce) can asparagus tips
Milk
1/3 cup butter or margarine
1/2 cup flour
1/2 teaspoon salt
1 pimento, chopped
4 hard-boiled eggs, sliced
3/4 cup (3 ounces) shredded Cheddar cheese
3/4 cup dry bread crumbs

Drain the asparagus, reserving the liquid. Pour the liquid into a 2-cup measure and fill with enough milk to make 2 cups. Melt the butter in a skillet. Whisk in the flour and salt. Add the asparagus and milk mixture gradually. Cook over low heat until the sauce thickens, stirring constantly. Remove from the heat. Stir in the pimento. Layer the asparagus, eggs, sauce and cheese in a greased 11/2-quart casserole. Top with the bread crumbs. Bake at 400 degrees for 20 minutes or until the mixture is bubbly and heated through.

Yield: 4 to 6 servings

Cindy Herring, Assistant Executive Director

Holiday Asparagus

2 (14-ounce) cans asparagus, drained
1/2 cup slivered almonds
1 (10-ounce) can cream of mushroom soup
1 cup (4 ounces) shredded Cheddar cheese
Stuffing mix or bread crumbs

Layer 1/2 of the asparagus and 1/2 of the almonds in a small casserole. Repeat the layers.

Combine the mushroom soup and cheese in a saucepan. Cook until the cheese melts, stirring constantly. Pour over the casserole.

Top with the stuffing mix. Bake at 350 degrees for 30 minutes.

Yield: 4 or 5 servings

Catherine Koehler, Trainer

Green Bean Casserole

2 (16-ounce) cans green beans, drained
1 (10-ounce) can cream of mushroom soup
1 teaspoon lemon juice
1 cup canned French-fried onions

Place the green beans in a greased casserole. Pour the cream of mushroom soup over the beans. Sprinkle the lemon juice over the soup.

Bake at 350 degrees for 30 minutes. Sprinkle the French-fried onions over the casserole. Bake for 5 minutes longer.

Yield: 6 servings

Adrianna Mell, Troop #29

Girl Scout Trivia
Juliette Gordon Low once sold her jewelry to fund the Girl Scout movement after 1914 when war broke out in Europe.

Marinated Green Beans

3 garlic cloves, crushed
Salt
1 cup vinegar
$1/3$ cup vegetable oil
2 cans green beans, drained
$1/2$ onion, sliced and separated into rings
1 large can whole or sliced mushrooms

Combine the garlic with enough salt in a bowl to make of paste consistency. Whisk in the vinegar and oil. Combine the beans, onion and mushrooms in a bowl. Pour the vinegar mixture over the vegetables and mix well. Let stand at room temperature for 1 hour. Chill until serving time. Will keep in the refrigerator for up to 1 week.

Yield: 4 to 6 servings

Cindy Herring, Assistant Executive Director

Sweet-and-Sour Green Beans

10 slices bacon
6 tablespoons sugar
6 tablespoons vinegar
2 cans cut or French-style green beans, drained
1 large purple onion, sliced
Slivered almonds

Cook the bacon in a skillet until crisp; drain, reserving the drippings. Crumble the bacon. Add the sugar and vinegar to the drippings in the skillet and mix well.

Layer the beans, onion, almonds and bacon 1/2 at a time in a casserole. Marinate, covered, in the refrigerator for 8 to 10 hours. Bake at 350 degrees for 45 minutes.

Yield: 10 to 12 servings

Amy Bole, Brownie Troop #275

Broccoli Casserole

2 eggs, beaten
1 (10-ounce) can cream of mushroom soup
1 cup (4 ounces) shredded Cheddar cheese
1 cup mayonnaise
2 packages frozen broccoli, cooked and drained
Butter crackers, crushed

Combine the eggs, cream of mushroom soup, cheese and mayonnaise in a bowl and mix well. Stir in the broccoli. Pour 1/2 of the broccoli mixture into a greased casserole. Add a layer of cracker crumbs. Top with the remaining broccoli mixture and another layer of cracker crumbs. Bake at 350 degrees for 30 minutes.

Yield: 8 servings

Rotsha Sanders, Troop #29

Cabbage Casserole

1¹/4 pounds ground beef
1 medium onion, chopped
2 ribs celery, chopped
1 medium green bell pepper, chopped
2 tablespoons Worcestershire sauce
1 teaspoon salt
1/2 teaspoon pepper
1 medium cabbage, chopped
Salt to taste
1/2 cup uncooked rice
2 cans stewed tomatoes

Combine the ground beef, chopped onion, celery, bell pepper,
Worcestershire sauce, 1 teaspoon salt and the pepper in a skillet.
Cook until the ground beef is browned, stirring until crumbly;
drain. Place the cabbage in a greased casserole. Sprinkle with salt
to taste.

Layer the ground beef mixture, rice and tomatoes over the
cabbage. Bake at 375 degrees for 1 hour.

Yield: 8 to 10 servings

Mary Alice Cates, Executive Director

Copper Pennies

1 (10-ounce) can tomato soup
1/2 cup vegetable oil
1 cup sugar
3/4 cup vinegar
1 tablespoon prepared mustard
1 tablespoon Worcestershire sauce
Salt to taste
5 cups cooked sliced carrots
1 green bell pepper, sliced
1 onion, sliced

Combine the tomato soup, oil, sugar, vinegar, mustard, Worcestershire sauce and salt in a saucepan. Bring to a boil, stirring constantly. Pour over the carrots, bell pepper and onion in a bowl.

Chill thoroughly. Will keep in the refrigerator for up to 2 weeks. Serve hot or cold.

Yield: 4 servings

Mary O. Crowe, Leader, 1960-65

Corn Fritters

**2 cups fresh corn kernels, or
    1 can cream-style corn**
1 egg, beaten
1 1/2 teaspoons sugar
1/3 teaspoon salt
1/8 teaspoon pepper
1 tablespoon margarine, melted
1/4 cup self-rising flour
1/2 teaspoon baking powder
Vegetable oil

Combine the corn, egg, sugar, salt, pepper and margarine in a bowl and mix well. Add a mixture of the flour and baking powder and mix well.

Heat a small amount of oil in a skillet. Drop by tablespoonfuls into the hot oil. Cook until golden brown on both sides.

Yield: 8 to 10 servings

Nancy Jackson, Product Sales Manager

Stuffed Eggplant

2 large eggplant
Olive oil
1 cup chopped green onions
Chopped fresh parsley
Salt and pepper to taste
6 tablespoons butter
1 pound lump crab meat
Bread crumbs
Grated Parmesan cheese

Cut the eggplant into halves lengthwise. Rub the cut surfaces with olive oil and place cut side down in a roasting pan. Bake at 350 degrees for 30 minutes. Scoop the pulp into a bowl, leaving 1/2-inch shells. Cook the green onions with a generous amount of parsley, salt and pepper in the butter in a skillet until the green onions are tender. Stir in the eggplant pulp. Simmer for a few minutes longer. Add the crab meat and mix well. Spoon into the eggplant shells. Sprinkle with bread crumbs and cheese. Bake at 350 degrees for 30 minutes.

Yield: 4 servings

Sheila Chandler, Program Director

Hot Greens

2 large packages frozen greens
Salt to taste
2 garlic cloves
2 tablespoons olive oil
1 can tomatoes with green chiles

Place the greens in a large saucepan. Add enough water to cover and salt to taste. Brown the garlic in the olive oil in a skillet. Add to the greens. Stir in the tomatoes with green chiles.

Cook until the greens are tender, stirring occasionally.

Yield: 8 to 10 servings

Nancy Jackson, Product Sales

Girl Scout Trivia
Juliette Gordon Low died in 1927. In the final paragraph of her will, she wrote "I leave and bequeath to my family my friendships, especially beloved Girl Scouts."

Southern Fried Okra

2 cups cornmeal
2 teaspoons salt, or to taste
2 teaspoons pepper
1 pound okra, cut into 1/2-inch pieces
1/2 cup vegetable oil

Combine the cornmeal, salt and pepper in a shallow bowl. Coat the okra with the cornmeal mixture.

Heat the oil in a skillet. Fry the okra in batches in the hot oil until brown and crisp, turning to cook evenly. Drain on paper towels.

Yield: 6 servings

Wanda Perry, Council Receptionist

Girl Scout Trivia
Robert Baden-Powell, the founder of the Boy Scouts, and his sister, Agnes, and wife, Olave, inspired Juliette Gordon Low to start the Girl Scouts in the U.S.

Peas and Okra

4 cups fresh field peas
1¹/₂ cups water
1 tablespoon salt
¹/₄ teaspoon pepper
¹/₄ pound salt pork
1 teaspoon sugar (optional)
8 okra pods

Combine the field peas, water, salt, pepper, salt pork and sugar in a saucepan. Bring to a boil.

Reduce the heat and simmer, covered, for 30 minutes. Add the okra. Cook for 15 minutes longer or until the vegetables are tender.

Yield: 4 to 7 servings

Wanda Perry, Council Receptionist

New Potatoes in White Sauce

3 cups peeled new potatoes
2 tablespoons cornstarch
2 cups milk
1/4 cup (1/2 stick) margarine
1/2 teaspoon salt
1/2 teaspoon pepper

Combine the potatoes with enough water to cover in a saucepan. Bring to a boil. Boil until tender; drain. Combine the cornstarch and milk in a saucepan and mix well. Add the margarine, salt and pepper.

Bring to a boil over medium heat. Boil for 1 minute, stirring constantly. Pour the sauce over the potatoes in a serving dish.

Yield: 4 to 5 servings

Sheila Chandler, Program Director

Potato Casserole

- 1 large package hash brown potatoes
- 1 (10-ounce) can cream of mushroom soup
- 1 (10-ounce) can chicken soup
- 1 (10-ounce) can cream of celery soup
- 1 medium onion, chopped
- 1 large bag shredded sharp Cheddar cheese
- 1 can mushrooms
- 1 can French-fried onion rings

Combine the hash brown potatoes, cream of mushroom soup, chicken soup, cream of celery soup, onion, cheese and mushrooms in a bowl and mix well. Spoon into a greased casserole.

Bake at 350 degrees for 30 minutes or until bubby. Top with the French-fried onion rings.

Yield: 6 to 8 servings

Lisa Adams, Troop #275

Ro-Tel Potatoes

8 to 10 potatoes, peeled and sliced
Salt to taste
1 green bell pepper, chopped
1 onion, chopped
1/2 cup (1 stick) butter or margarine
1 pound Velveeta cheese, cubed
1 small can mushrooms
1 can Ro-Tel tomatoes

Combine the potatoes with enough salted water to cover in a saucepan. Bring to a boil. Boil until tender; drain. Place the potatoes in a greased 9×13-inch baking dish. Sauté the bell pepper and onion in the butter in a skillet until tender. Add the Velveeta cheese. Cook over medium heat until the cheese melts, stirring constantly. Stir in the mushrooms and tomatoes. Pour over the potatoes. Bake at 350 degrees for 10 to 20 minutes or until bubbly.

Yield: 10 servings

Arnecia Lee, Troop #122

Spinach Squares

1 cup flour
1 teaspoon salt
1 teaspoon baking powder
1 cup milk
1/4 cup (1/2 stick) butter, melted
2 eggs, beaten
1 package frozen chopped spinach, cooked and drained
1 medium onion, chopped
2 cups (8 ounces) shredded sharp Cheddar cheese
2 cups (8 ounces) shredded Monterey Jack cheese

Sift the flour, salt and baking powder into a bowl. Add the milk, butter and eggs and mix well. Stir in the spinach, onion, Cheddar cheese and Monterey Jack cheese. Pour into a lightly greased 9x13-inch baking pan. Bake at 350 degrees for 35 to 40 minutes. Cut into squares.

Yield: 15 to 20 servings

Note: This dish makes a great appetizer as well as a side dish. It freezes well, too.

Mary Alice Cates, Executive Director

Delta Squash

1 pound yellow squash, sliced
1 small onion, chopped
2 cups water
1 tablespoon butter
1 cup shredded cheese
1 cup milk
1/2 cup bread crumbs
2 egg yolks
1/2 teaspoon salt
1/2 teaspoon pepper
2 egg whites

Cook the squash and onion in the water in a saucepan until tender; drain. Add the butter. Mash thoroughly. Add the cheese, milk, bread crumbs, egg yolks, salt and pepper and mix well. Beat the egg whites in a mixing bowl until stiff peaks form. Fold into the squash mixture. Spoon into a greased baking dish. Bake at 350 degrees for 30 minutes or until light brown.

Yield: 4 to 6 servings

Annie Roby, Field Executive

Squash Casserole

1 pound squash, sliced
1 onion, chopped
1 carrot, chopped
1 cup sour cream
1 (10-ounce) can cream of chicken soup
1/2 cup (1 stick) margarine, melted
2 cups herb-seasoned stuffing mix

Bring enough water to cover the squash, onion and carrot to a boil in a saucepan. Add the vegetables. Cook until tender; drain. Combine the vegetables, sour cream and cream of chicken soup in a bowl and mix well. Combine the margarine and stuffing mix in a bowl and mix well. Layer 1/2 of the squash mixture and 1/2 of the stuffing mixture in a greased 9×13-inch baking dish. Top with the remaining squash mixture and stuffing mixture. Bake at 350 degrees for 45 minutes.

Yield: 4 to 6 servings

Mary Alice Cates, Executive Director

Sweet Potato Casserole

2 cups mashed cooked sweet potatoes
2 eggs, beaten
3/4 cup (11/2 sticks) margarine, melted
11/4 cups sugar
1/4 cup flour
1/2 cup packed brown sugar
1/2 cup chopped pecans
1/2 cup flaked or shredded coconut
1 cup cornflakes

Combine the sweet potatoes, eggs, margarine and a mixture of the sugar and flour in a large bowl and mix well. Pour into a greased shallow casserole.

Combine the brown sugar, pecans, coconut and cornflakes in a small bowl and mix well. Sprinkle over the sweet potato mixture. Bake at 350 degrees for 30 minutes or until set.

Yield: 4 to 6 servings

Nancy Jackson, Product Sales

Sweet Potato Cups

6 medium sweet potatoes
4 oranges
1/2 cup packed light brown sugar
2 tablespoons butter or margarine
1 teaspoon nutmeg
1/2 teaspoon cinnamon
1/2 teaspoon vanilla extract
1/4 teaspoon salt

Combine the sweet potatoes with enough water to cover in a large saucepan. Bring to a boil. Boil until tender; drain. Peel the sweet potatoes and cut into chunks. Cut the oranges into halves. Squeeze 1/4 cup orange juice. Combine the juice and the sweet potatoes in a large mixing bowl. Beat until fluffy. Add the brown sugar, butter, nutmeg, cinnamon, vanilla and salt and mix well. Remove the pulp from the orange halves. Fill the halves with the sweet potato mixture, using a spoon or a pastry bag. Place the filled sweet potato cups on a baking sheet. Bake at 350 degrees for 20 to 25 minutes. Arrange around a turkey, if desired. Garnish with parsley.

Yield: 8 servings

Querrida Johnson, Troop #162

Turnip Green Casserole

**1 (15-ounce) can chopped turnip greens or
    mustard greens**
1 teaspoon sugar
Salt and pepper to taste
1/2 (10-ounce) can cream of mushroom soup
1/2 cup mayonnaise
2 tablespoons wine vinegar
1 teaspoon prepared horseradish
2 eggs, lightly beaten
Bread crumbs
Shredded Cheddar cheese

Combine the turnip greens, sugar, salt, pepper, cream of
mushroom soup, mayonnaise, vinegar, horseradish and eggs
in a bowl and mix well. Pour into a greased casserole. Top with
bread crumbs and shredded Cheddar cheese. Bake at 350 degrees
for 1 hour.

Yield: 6 to 8 servings

Note: This dish multiplies well for a big crowd.

Andie O'Bryant, Troop #8

Fried Green Tomatoes

2 eggs
2 cups yellow cornmeal
Salt and pepper to taste
4 green tomatoes, thickly sliced
2 cups vegetable oil

Beat the eggs in a shallow dish. Combine the cornmeal, salt and pepper on a plate and and mix well. Dip the tomato slices in the egg. Coat with the cornmeal mixture.

Heat the oil in a cast-iron skillet. Fry the tomatoes in the hot oil for 3 minutes or until golden brown, turning once.

Yield: 6 to 8 servings

Sheila Chandler, Program Director

Girl Scout Trivia
A Girl Scout can learn more about her individual faith by pursuing a religious recognition.

Poppy's Macaroni and Cheese

1 large package bow tie pasta
1 1/2 pounds Velveeta cheese, cubed
Milk
Salt and pepper to taste

Cook the pasta using the package directions; drain. Melt the Velveeta cheese with a small amount of milk in a saucepan over low heat, stirring constantly until creamy. Add the hot pasta, salt and pepper and mix well.

Yield: 4 to 6 servings

Katie Wilson, Carrollton Brownies, Troop #275

Corn Bread Dressing

3 cups chopped onions
3 cups chopped celery
1 tablespoon olive oil
1 cup (2 sticks) unsalted butter, melted
1 recipe Corn Bread for Dressing (page 193)
1/2 to 1 cup chopped fresh sage
1 1/2 teaspoons salt, or to taste
1/2 teaspoon pepper, or to taste
2 cups turkey stock or canned chicken broth

Cook the onions and celery in the olive oil and 2 tablespoons of the butter in a large skillet for 7 minutes or until tender. Pour into a large bowl. Crumble the corn bread. Add the corn bread, sage, salt and pepper to the onion mixture and mix well. Spoon into a greased 9×13-inch baking dish. Drizzle the remaining butter over the corn bread mixture. Pour the turkey stock over the top. Bake, covered, at 350 degrees for 20 minutes. Uncover and bake for 10 minutes longer.

Yield: 15 to 20 servings

Breshia Barnes, Troop #259

Corn Bread

1/2 cup vegetable oil
2 cups stone-ground cornmeal
2 cups flour
2 tablespoons baking powder
1/4 cup sugar
1 teaspoon salt, or to taste
2 eggs, lightly beaten
2 cups milk

Pour the oil into a 9×13-inch baking pan. Heat in the oven at 450 degrees for 5 minutes or until very hot. Combine the cornmeal, flour, baking powder, sugar and salt in a large bowl and mix well. Add the eggs and milk and mix well. Pour carefully into the heated pan. Bake at 450 degrees for 20 to 25 minutes or until golden brown. Let stand for 10 minutes.

Yield: 15 to 20 servings

Seasoned Brown Rice

2 cups chicken broth
1 cup brown rice
2 tablespoons minced onion
1 tablespoon butter
1 garlic clove, minced
3 sprigs of parsley
1/4 teaspoon thyme
1 bay leaf
1/8 teaspoon cayenne pepper
1/2 teaspoon salt

Combine the chicken broth, brown rice, onion, butter, garlic, parsley, thyme, bay leaf, cayenne pepper and salt in a greased casserole.

Bake, covered, at 350 degrees for 45 to 60 minutes. Discard the parsley and the bay leaf. Serve with chicken, meat loaf or fish.

Yield: 4 to 6 servings

Querrida Johnson, Troop #162

Grandma's Cheese Grits

4 cups water
1 teaspoon salt
1 cup grits
1/2 cup (1 stick) butter
1 roll garlic cheese, chopped
2 eggs

Bring the water and salt to a boil in a saucepan. Stir in the grits. Cook for 7 to 8 minutes, stirring occasionally. Add the butter and stir until melted. Add the garlic cheese and stir until melted. Remove from the heat. Add the eggs and stir vigorously. Pour into a buttered casserole. Bake, uncovered, at 350 degrees for 15 minutes.

Yield: 4 to 6 servings

Note: These grits are excellent with pork or chicken dishes.

Opal Cornacchione, Troop #115

Sweets

Baking Secrets

- ❖ When a cake recipe calls for flouring the baking pan, use a bit of the dry cake mix instead. This will eliminate messy bits of flour on the outside of the cake.

- ❖ For perfectly shaped cakes or jelly rolls, first grease the pan, then line it with greased waxed paper. After baking, invert the pan and peel off the waxed paper. You'll have no more broken corners or edges. Use this technique for fudges and bars as well.

- ❖ To prevent icing from running off your cake, try dusting the surface lightly with cornstarch before icing.

- ❖ When filling and frosting a cake, place first layer(s) with the bottom side up; place the last layer with the top side up.

- ❖ A handy substitute for cake flour: 1 cup minus 2 tablespoons of all-purpose flour equals 1 cup cake flour.

- ❖ Always use whole milk rather than skim or reduced-fat milk in your pastry recipes.

- ❖ The sharp open ends of clean cans make great biscuit, scone, and cookie cutters.

- ❖ Brush beaten egg white over pie pastry before baking to yield a beautiful glossy finish.

- ❖ Two sure-fire ways to keep meringue toppings from shrinking: First, spread the meringue while the pie filling is hot. Second, make sure the meringue touches the crust all around.

Apricot Upside-Down Cake

1/4 cup (1/2 stick) butter or margarine, melted
1/3 cup packed light brown sugar
1 (17-ounce) can apricot halves packed in juice
1/2 cup pecan halves
2/3 cup sugar
1/3 cup butter or margarine, softened
1 egg
1 teaspoon vanilla extract
1 teaspoon grated orange zest
1 1/2 cups cake flour
2 1/2 teaspoons baking powder
1/4 teaspoon salt
1/2 cup chopped dried apricots

Combine 1/4 cup melted butter and the brown sugar in a bowl and mix well. Spread in a 9-inch cake pan. Drain the apricots, reserving 2/3 cup juice. Slice the apricots. Arrange the apricots and pecans over the brown sugar mixture. Cream the sugar and 1/3 cup butter in a mixing bowl until light and fluffy. Beat in the egg, vanilla and orange zest. Combine the flour, baking powder and salt in a bowl. Add to the creamed mixture alternately with the reserved apricot juice, blending well after each addition. Stir in the dried apricots. Spread the batter over the apricot layer in the pan. Bake at 350 degrees for 40 to 45 minutes or until a wooden pick inserted near the center comes out clean. Cook for 5 minutes longer. Invert onto a serving plate.

Yield: 8 servings

Desiree Orange, Troop #25

Apple Dapple Cake

3 eggs
1½ cups vegetable oil
2 cups sugar
2 teaspoons vanilla extract
3 cups flour
1 teaspoon salt
1 teaspoon baking soda
3 cups chopped apples
1½ cups pecans, chopped
Brown Sugar Topping (below)

Combine the eggs, oil, sugar, vanilla, flour, salt, baking soda, apples and pecans in a large bowl and mix well. Pour into a greased and floured tube pan. Bake at 350 degrees for 1 hour and 20 minutes or until the cake tests done. Cool in the pan for 10 minutes. Invert onto a serving plate. Pour Brown Sugar Topping over the hot cake.

Yield: 16 servings

Brown Sugar Topping

1 cup packed brown sugar
1/2 cup (1 stick) margarine
1/4 cup milk

Combine the brown sugar, margarine and milk in a saucepan. Cook over low heat until the brown sugar has dissolved, stirring constantly until smooth.

Nancy Jackson, Product Sales Manager

Banana Cake

1 (2-layer) package yellow cake mix
1/2 cup water
3/4 cup vegetable oil
2 eggs
2 cups mashed bananas
1 teaspoon baking soda
Caramel Glaze (below)

Combine the cake mix, water, oil and eggs in a bowl and mix well.
Combine the bananas and baking soda in a small bowl. Add to the
creamed mixture and mix well. Pour into a greased and floured
bundt pan. Bake at 350 degrees for 35 to 40 minutes or until
the cake tests done. Cool in the pan for 10 minutes. Invert onto
a serving plate. Pour Caramel Icing over the hot cake.

Yield: 16 servings

Nancy Jackson, Product Sales

Caramel Icing

1/2 cup (1 stick) margarine
1 cup packed brown sugar
1/4 cup milk
2 1/2 cups confectioners' sugar
1 teaspoon vanilla extract
1 cup chopped nuts

Combine the margarine and brown sugar in a saucepan. Cook
over low heat until the brown sugar has dissolved, stirring constantly
until smooth. Add the remaining ingredients and mix well.

Fruit Cocktail Cake

2 cups flour
11/2 cups sugar
2 teaspoons baking soda
1/2 teaspoon salt
2 eggs
1 (16-ounce) can fruit cocktail
Coconut
Brown sugar
Vanilla Icing (below)

Combine the flour, sugar, baking soda, salt, eggs and fruit cocktail in a bowl and mix well. Pour into a greased and floured 9×13-inch cake pan. Sprinkle coconut and brown sugar over the top. Bake at 300 degrees for 1 hour. Spread the Vanilla Icing over the warm cake.

Yield: 15 servings

Vanilla Icing

1/2 cup (1 stick) margarine, softened
3/4 cup sugar
1/2 cup evaporated milk
1 teaspoon vanilla

Cream the margarine and sugar in a mixing bowl until light and fluffy. Beat in the evaporated milk and vanilla.

Janet Young, Leader, Troop #7

Lemon Apricot Cake

1 (2-layer) package lemon supreme cake mix
1/2 cup sugar
3/4 cup vegetable oil
1 cup apricot nectar
4 eggs
Lemon Glaze (below)

Combine the cake mix, sugar, oil and apricot nectar in a mixing bowl and mix well. Add the eggs 1 at a time, mixing well after each addition. Pour into a greased and floured bundt pan. Bake at 325 degrees for 1 hour. Cool in the pan for 10 minutes. Invert onto a serving plate. Pour the Lemon Glaze over the warm cake.

Yield: 10 servings

Lemon Glaze

1 cup confectioners' sugar
Juice of 1 to 2 lemons

Combine the confectioners' sugar and the lemon juice in a bowl and mix well.

Mary Kathryn Quigley, Troop #97

Caramel Cake

1 (2-layer) package yellow cake mix
2 eggs
1/4 cup vegetable oil
1/2 teaspoon vanilla extract
1/2 cup self-rising cake flour
Caramel Icing (below)

Mix the cake mix, eggs, oil, vanilla and flour in a bowl. Spoon into two 9-inch cake pans. Bake according to the package directions for two 9-inch pans. Let the cake cool completely. Spread Caramel Icing between the layers and over the top layer of the cake.

Yield: 12 to 15 servings

Caramel Icing

1 (14-ounce) can sweetened condensed milk

Pour the condensed milk into a pie plate and cover with foil. Place the pie plate in a larger baking pan. Add enough hot water to the baking pan to come partway up the side of the pie plate. Bake at 425 degrees for 1 hour or until thick and caramel colored.

Sheila Rush, Troop #122

Butterfinger Cake

   1 (2-layer) package yellow cake mix
   1 (14-ounce) can sweetened condensed milk
   4 Butterfinger candy bars, crushed
   1 (8-ounce) container whipped topping

Prepare and bake the cake mix using the package directions for a 9×13-inch cake pan. Pour the condensed milk over the warm cake. Sprinkle 2 crushed candy bars over the condensed milk. Let stand until cool. Top with the whipped topping and the remaining 2 crushed candy bars.

Yield: 15 servings

Jennifer Meredith, Leader, Troop #336

Chocolate Chip Cake

   1 (2-layer) package yellow cake mix
   1 (4-ounce) package chocolate instant pudding mix
   4 eggs
   3/4 cup vegetable oil
   1 tablespoon vanilla extract
   1 cup (6 ounces) chocolate chips

Mix the first 5 ingredients in a mixing bowl. Stir in the chocolate chips. Spoon into a bundt pan coated with nonstick cooking spray. Bake at 350 degrees for 50 minutes. Cool in the pan for 10 to 15 minutes. Invert onto a wire rack to cool completely.

Yield: 10 to 12 servings

Anna Frances Morgan, Troop #97

Mississippi Mud Cake

2 cups sugar
1 1/2 cups flour
1/2 cup baking cocoa
1/4 teaspoon salt
3 eggs
1 cup (2 sticks) unsalted
    butter, melted

1 cup chopped pecans
1 tablespoon vanilla extract
2 cups miniature
    marshmallows
Chocolate-Pecan Icing
    (below)
1/2 cup chopped pecans

Combine the sugar, flour, baking cocoa and salt in a mixing bowl. Beat in the eggs 1 at a time. Stir in the butter, 1 cup pecans and the vanilla. Pour into a buttered 9×13-inch cake pan. Bake at 350 degrees for 25 to 30 minutes. Sprinkle the marshmallows over the hot cake. Return the cake to the oven until the marshmallows are softened. Spread the Chocolate-Pecan Icing over the warm cake. Sprinkle with 1/2 cup pecans.

Yield: 15 servings

Chocolate-Pecan Icing

1 (1-pound) package
    confectioners' sugar
1/3 cup baking cocoa
1 cup (2 sticks) unsalted
    butter, melted

1 to 2 tablespoons
    evaporated milk
1 teaspoon vanilla extract
1 cup chopped pecans

Combine the sugar and baking cocoa in a mixing bowl. Add the next 3 ingredients and beat until light and fluffy. Stir in the pecans.

Note: This cake was prepared at my home in Greenville for a cake cook-off and was filmed for *FoodNation* with Bobby Flay.

Sue Seratt, Field Executive

Fudge Cake

1 (2-layer) package dark chocolate cake mix
1/2 cup chocolate syrup
1/2 cup sugar
Chocolate Icing (below)

Prepare and bake the cake mix using the package directions for a
9×13-inch cake pan. Combine the chocolate syrup and sugar in a
saucepan. Cook over low heat until the sugar is dissolved, stirring
constantly. Pour over the warm cake. Top with Chocolate Icing.
Serve hot.

Yield: 25 servings

Chocolate Icing

1/2 cup (1 stick) butter, melted
1/4 cup baking cocoa
1 teaspoon vanilla extract
5 cups confectioners' sugar
1 (12-ounce) can evaporated milk

Combine the melted butter, baking cocoa, vanilla, 1/2 of the
confectioners' sugar and 1/3 of the evaporated milk in a mixing
bowl. Beat until smooth. Add the remaining sugar and additional
evaporated milk, 1 teaspoon at a time, to make of spreading
consistency.

Jennifer Meredith, Troop Leader

Cool Whip Coconut Cake

1 (2-layer) package white cake mix
2 (14-ounce) cans sweetened condensed milk
1 (12-ounce) can evaporated milk
1 (16-ounce) container Cool Whip
1 large package shredded or flaked coconut (not frozen)

Prepare and bake the cake mix using the package directions for two 9-inch cake pans. Cool in the pans for 10 minutes. Remove 1 layer to a serving plate. Pierce the cake at regular intervals with a wooden pick.

Combine the condensed milk and evaporated milk in a bowl and mix well. Pour 1/2 of the milk mixture over the holes in the cake, pouring slowly to allow absorption of the liquid.

Spread a layer of Cool Whip over the cake layer. Top with the remaining cake layer. Pierce with a wooden pick. Pour the remaining milk mixture over the cake. Spread the remaining Cool Whip over the top and side of the cake. Sprinkle the top and side with coconut. Store the cake in the refrigerator.

Yield: 12 servings

Council Recipe

Jell-O Picnic Cake

1 (2-layer) package white cake mix
1 (3-ounce) package lemon-flavored Jell-O
1 cup boiling water
1 (8-ounce) container whipped topping

Prepare and bake the cake mix using the package directions for a 9×13-inch cake pan. Pierce the cake at regular intervals with a wooden pick.

Dissolve the Jell-O in the water in a heatproof bowl. Let stand until cool. Pour over the cake, pouring slowly to allow absorption of the liquid. Chill in the refrigerator until cool.

Frost with the whipped topping. Store the cake in the refrigerator.

Yield: 12 servings

Lynn Lambert, Troop #115

Girl Scout Trivia
The Girl Scout handbook was transcribed into Braille and large type in 1933.

Peanut Butter and Banana Cake

3 cups flour
11/2 cups sugar
1/2 cup buttermilk
1/2 cup (1 stick) margarine, softened
3 eggs
2 teaspoons vanilla extract
6 bananas
1/2 cup sugar
Peanut Butter Icing (below)

Combine the flour, sugar, buttermilk, margarine, eggs and vanilla in a mixing bowl. Beat until smooth and creamy. Slice two of the bananas and spread them in a greased 1/2-sheet cake pan. Pour the batter over the bananas. Bake at 350 degrees for 35 minutes. Mash the 4 remaining bananas with 1/2 cup sugar and spread over the cake. Top with Peanut Butter Icing.

Yield: 25 servings

Peanut Butter Icing

1 cup peanut butter
1 cup evaporated milk
1 cup sugar

Combine the peanut butter, evaporated milk and sugar in a saucepan. Cook over low heat until smooth and creamy, stirring constantly.

Jennifer Meredith, Troop Leader

Seven-Up Pound Cake

1½ cups (3 sticks) butter, softened
3 cups sugar
5 eggs

3 cups flour
2 tablespoons lemon flavoring
3/4 cup Seven-Up

Cream the butter and sugar in a mixing bowl until light and fluffy. Beat in the eggs 1 at a time. Add the flour and mix well. Stir in the lemon flavoring and Seven-Up. Pour into a greased and floured bundt pan. Bake at 325 degrees for 1 to 1¼ hours.

Yield: 6 servings

Shaquana Kimble, Troop #122

Old-Fashioned Butter Pound Cake

1 pound (4 sticks) butter, softened
2½ cups sugar
9 eggs

3 cups flour
1 teaspoon each cream of tartar and lemon flavoring

Cream the butter and sugar in a mixing bowl until light and fluffy. Beat in the eggs 1 at a time. Add the flour and cream of tartar gradually, mixing well after each addition. Stir in the lemon flavoring. Pour into a greased and floured tube pan. Bake at 350 degrees for 1 hour or until the cake tests done.

Yield: 12 servings

Rashikiyana Ball, Troop #122

Elma's Sour Cream Pound Cake

1 cup (2 sticks) butter or margarine, softened
3 cups sugar
6 eggs
3 cups flour
1/4 teaspoon baking soda
1/4 teaspoon salt
1 cup sour cream
2 teaspoons vanilla extract

Cream the butter and sugar in a mixing bowl until light and fluffy. Add the eggs 1 at a time, beating well after each addition. Sift the flour 2 times. Add the baking soda and salt to the flour and sift again.

Add to the creamed mixture alternately with the sour cream, mixing well after each addition. Stir in the vanilla. Pour into a greased and floured tube pan.

Bake at 325 degrees for 1 hour and 25 minutes or until the cake tests done. Cool in the pan for 15 minutes. Invert onto a serving plate.

Yield: 20 servings

Elma Reed, Leader, Troop #118

Girl Scout Trivia

Wider Opportunities are offered to Cadette and Senior Girl Scouts. These are experiences that go beyond the troop setting. They can broaden your horizons by enabling you to meet new people, travel to new places, or try new activities.

Panic Cake

1 (21-ounce) can favorite pie filling
1 (2-layer) package yellow cake mix
1 cup (2 sticks) margarine, melted
1/2 cup chopped nuts

Pour the pie filling into a greased 9×13-inch cake pan. Sprinkle the dry cake mix over the pie filling. Pour the margarine over the top. Top with the nuts. Bake at 350 degrees for 30 to 43 minutes.

Yield: 15 servings

Konnie Brewer, Troop #275

Caramel Icing

2 cups sugar
2 cups heavy cream or evaporated milk
1 to 11/2 tablespoons butter
1 teaspoon vanilla extract

Combine 11/2 cups of the sugar with the cream in a saucepan. Bring to a boil. Reduce the heat and simmer. Heat the remaining 1/2 cup sugar in a skillet. Cook over medium-high heat until the sugar browns, stirring constantly. Stir into the cream mixture. Cook, uncovered, over medium heat to 234 to 240 degrees on a candy thermometer, soft-ball stage, stirring frequently. Remove from the heat. Beat in the butter and vanilla. Cool slightly before spreading.

Yield: Enough icing for one 2-layer cake

Nahdra Curry, Troop #76

Lemon Cake Icing

1 1/2 cups sugar
1/2 cup (1 stick) margarine
3 large eggs, lightly beaten
Juice of 3 lemons

Combine the sugar, margarine, eggs and lemon juice in the top of a double boiler. Cook over low heat for 12 minutes or until smooth and thickened, stirring constantly. Remove from the heat. Cool slightly before spreading.

Yield: Enough icing for one 2-layer cake

Danisha Williams, Troop #252

Mama's Powdered Sugar Icing

Confectioners' sugar
1/2 teaspoon vanilla extract
Milk
Raspberry- or strawberry-flavored gelatin

Pour the desired amount of confectioners' sugar into a bowl. Beat in the vanilla and enough milk to make of spreading consistency. Add a small amount of the gelatin to add flavor and color.

Yield: variable

Note: This is Kelsey Stephens's great-grandmother's recipe. She is 100 years old!

Kelsey Stephens, Troop #97

Apple Pie

1/2 cup sugar
1/2 cup self-rising flour
1 teaspoon cinnamon
1/2 cup (1 stick) butter, softened
1/2 cup packed brown sugar
1 can apple pie filling
1 unbaked (10-inch) deep-dish pie shell

Combine the sugar, flour and cinnamon in a bowl. Combine the butter and brown sugar in a bowl and mix well. Spread 1/2 of the apple pie filling in the pie shell. Sprinkle with 1/2 of the cinnamon mixture.

Top with the remaining pie filling. Sprinkle with the remaining cinnamon mixture. Dot with the brown sugar mixture. Bake at 375 degrees for 45 minutes.

Yield: 8 servings

Council Recipe

Girl Scout Trivia
During World War I and II, special programs on seafaring and aviation, called Mariner and Wing Girl Scouts, were launched for Senior Girl Scouts.

Blueberry Pie

1 (2-crust) pie pastry
5 cups fresh blueberries, or 2 (14-ounce)
packages frozen blueberries, thawed and drained
1 tablespoon lemon juice
1 to 2 teaspoons vanilla extract
1 cup sugar
1/3 cup flour (increase to 1/2 cup if using frozen
blueberries)
1/8 teaspoon salt
2 tablepoons butter
1 egg, lightly beaten
1 teaspoon sugar

Line a pie plate with 1 pastry. Sprinkle the blueberries with the lemon juice and vanilla in a large bowl. Combine 1 cup sugar, the flour and salt in a bowl. Add to the berries and mix well. Pour into the lined pie plate. Dot with the butter. Top with the remaining pastry, sealing the edge and cutting vents. Brush the pastry with the beaten egg. Sprinkle with 1 teaspoon sugar. Bake at 400 degrees for 35 minutes or until the crust is golden brown and the filling is bubbly.

Yield: 6 to 8 servings

Josephine Howard, Troop #97

Strawberry Pecan Pie

1 (14-ounce) can sweetened condensed milk
Juice of 2 lemons
2 cups sliced strawberries
1 cup chopped pecans
1 (8-ounce) container whipped topping
1 baked (9-inch) pie shell or graham cracker pie shell

Combine the condensed milk and lemon juice in a bowl. Let stand for 5 to 10 minutes. Add the strawberries and pecans.

Fold in the whipped topping. Pour into the pie shell. Chill for 2 to 3 hours.

Yield: 8 servings

Nancy Jackson, Product Sales Manager

Girl Scout Trivia
In the early days of Girl Scouting in the U.S., the girls made their own uniforms—long, dark skirts and blouses with blue ties.

Never-Fail Chocolate Pie

1 cup sugar
3 tablespoons flour
2 tablespoons baking cocoa
1 pinch of salt
1 cup milk
3 egg yolks, lightly beaten
1/4 cup (1/2 stick) butter
1 baked (9-inch) pie shell
Meringue (below)

Combine the sugar, flour, baking cocoa and salt in a bowl. Combine the milk, egg yolks and butter in a saucepan. Cook over medium heat until hot, stirring constantly until smooth. Whisk in the cocoa mixture. Pour into the pie shell. Top with the Meringue, sealing to the edge. Bake at 350 degrees for 12 to 15 minutes.

Yield: 6 to 8 servings

Meringue

3 egg whites
1/4 teaspoon cream of tartar
6 tablespoons sugar
1/2 teaspoon vanilla extract

Beat the egg whites with the cream of tartar in a mixing bowl until soft peaks form. Add the sugar gradually, beating constantly until stiff peaks form. Beat in the vanilla.

Yield: 6 to 8 servings

Anne Kristen Wigington, Troop #39

Triple Layer Mud Pie

2 ounces semisweet baking chocolate, melted
1/4 cup sweetened condensed milk
1 (9-inch) chocolate crumb pie shell
3/4 cup chopped pecans, toasted
2 cups cold milk
2 (4-ounce) packages chocolate instant
  pudding mix
1 (8-ounce) container whipped topping, thawed

Combine the chocolate and condensed milk in a bowl and mix well. Pour into the pie shell. Press the pecans evenly into the chocolate. Chill for 10 minutes.

Pour the milk into a large bowl. Add the pudding mixes and beat with a wire whisk for 2 minutes or until smooth. Spread 1 1/2 cups of the pudding over the chocolate layer in the pie shell. Stir 1/2 of the whipped topping into the remaining pudding. Spread over the pudding in the pie shell. Top with the remaining whipped topping. Chill for 3 hours or until set. Garnish as desired.

Yield: 8 servings.

Note: To toast pecans, spread them evenly on a baking sheet. Bake at 375 degrees for 3 to 5 minutes or until the pecans are well toasted.

J'Kea Starks, Troop #259

Chocolate Chip Pecan Pie

1 cup sugar
1/2 cup sifted flour
2 eggs, beaten
1/2 cup (1 stick) margarine, melted and cooled
1 cup chopped pecans
1 cup (6 ounces) semisweet chocolate chips
1 teaspoon vanilla extract
1 unbaked (9-inch) pie shell

Combine the sugar and flour in a mixing bowl. Add the eggs, margarine, pecans, chocolate chips and vanilla and mix well. Pour into the pie shell. Bake at 350 degrees for 40 to 45 minutes or until the top is crusty. Top each serving with a scoop of vanilla ice cream, if desired.

Yield: 8 servings

Nancy Jackson, Product Sales Manager

Chess Pie

3 eggs, beaten
2 cups sugar
1 cup milk
1/2 cup (1 stick) margarine, melted
2 tablespoons flour
1 teaspoon vanilla extract
1 unbaked (9-inch) pie shell

Combine the eggs, sugar, milk, margarine, flour and vanilla in a mixing bowl and mix well. Pour into the pie shell. Bake at 350 degrees for 1 hour or until a knife inserted near the center comes out clean.

Yield: 8 servings

Council Recipe

Egg Pie

2 eggs
1 cup milk
1 cup sugar
6 tablespoons butter, melted
1 teaspoon vanilla extract
1/2 teaspoon nutmeg
2 unbaked (9-inch) pie shells

Combine the eggs, milk, sugar, butter, vanilla and nutmeg in a mixing bowl. Beat at medium speed for 2 minutes. Divide the mixture between the 2 pie shells.

Bake at 300 degrees for 30 minutes. Let stand until cool.

Yield: 16 servings

Janice William, Troop #126

Girl Scout Trivia
February 22 is known as Thinking Day. On this day, girls exchange greetings and contribute to a special fund used to promote Girl Guiding and Girl Scouting throughout the world.

Lemon Pie

1 (14-ounce) can sweetened condensed milk
1/2 cup lemon juice
1 (8-ounce) container whipped topping
1 (9-inch) graham cracker pie shell

Combine the condensed milk and lemon juice in a bowl and mix well. Fold in the whipped topping. Pour into the pie shell. Chill for 2 to 3 hours.

Yield: 6 to 8 servings

Ebony Waters, Troop # 128

Lime Pie

1 (3-ounce) package lime-flavored gelatin
2 cups Key lime yogurt
1 (8-ounce) container whipped topping
1 (9-inch) graham cracker pie shell

Combine the gelatin and yogurt in a bowl and mix well. Fold in the whipped topping. Spread in the pie shell. Chill for 20 minutes or longer before serving. Garnish with a slice of Key lime and whipped topping.

Yield: 8 servings

Latiana Day, Troop # 128

Lemonade Pie

**1 (12-ounce) can frozen lemonade concentrate,
    partially thawed
1 (8-ounce) container whipped topping
1 (14-ounce) can sweetened condensed milk
2 (9-inch) graham cracker pie shells, or 1 deep-dish
    graham cracker pie shell**

Combine the lemonade concentrate, whipped topping and condensed milk in a large bowl and mix well. Pour into the pie shells.

Freeze, covered, for 3 hours or longer. Garnish with lemon slices or other sliced fruit.

Yield: 8 servings

Note: This is excellent on hot summer days.

Katie Wilson, Troop #275

Girl Scout Trivia

Girl Scouting is designed for all girls. The first troop of physically disabled girls was organized in 1917 at the School for Crippled Children in New York City.

Pecan Pie

1 cup sugar
1 cup light or dark corn syrup
1/4 cup (1/2 stick) butter, melted
2 tablespoons flour
3 eggs, lightly beaten
1 cup pecans, chopped or halved
2 teaspoons vanilla extract
1 unbaked (9-inch) pie shell

Combine the sugar, corn syrup, butter, flour, eggs, pecans and vanilla in the order listed in a mixing bowl, mixing well after each addition. Pour into the pie shell. Bake at 375 degrees for 1 1/4 hours.

Yield: 8 servings

Note: To make 2 pies, use 5 large eggs, 3 tablespoons flour and 1 tablespoon vanilla. Double the remaining ingredients. This doubled amount will also make about 8 small pies. I bake them on a baking sheet in the oven directly below the larger pies.

Jeanne LeBlanc, Troop #39

Pumpkin Cheesecake Pie

1 (12-ounce) package cream cheese, softened
1/2 cup sugar
11/2 teaspoons pumpkin pie spice
1 cup pumpkin
2 eggs, lightly beaten
1 (9-inch) graham cracker pie shell

Combine the cream cheese, sugar and pumpkin pie spice in a mixing bowl. Beat at medium speed until smooth. Stir in the pumpkin and eggs and mix well.

Pour into the pie shell. Bake at 350 degrees for 40 minutes. Let stand until cool. Chill for 3 hours or longer.

Yield: 8 servings

Moraysheal Jackson, Troop #259

Soda Cracker Pie

3 egg whites
Pinch of salt
1 cup sugar
1 teaspoon vanilla extract
3/4 cup crushed soda crackers
1 tablespoon baking powder
Whipped topping
3/4 cup chopped pecans

Beat the egg whites with the salt in a mixing bowl until soft peaks form. Add the sugar and vanilla gradually, beating constantly until stiff peaks form. Combine the soda crackers and baking powder in a bowl and mix well. Fold into the egg white mixture.

Pour into an ungreased pie plate. Bake at 325 degrees for 30 minutes. Let stand until cool. Spread whipped topping over the pie and sprinkle with the pecans.

Yield: 8 servings

Nancy Jackson, Product Sales Manager

Chocolate Delight

3/4 cup (1 1/2 sticks) margarine, softened
1 1/2 cups flour
1/2 cup chopped nuts
1 (8-ounce) package cream cheese, softened
1 cup confectioners' sugar
2 cups whipped topping
2 (4-ounce) packages vanilla instant pudding mix
1 (4-ounce) package chocolate instant pudding mix
5 cups milk
Whipped topping
Chopped nuts

Combine the margarine, flour and nuts in a bowl and mix well. Pat into a greased 9×13-inch baking dish. Bake at 325 degrees for 25 minutes. Let stand until cool.

Beat the cream cheese and confectioners' sugar in a mixing bowl until light and fluffy. Fold in the whipped topping. Spread over the baked crust. Combine the pudding mixes and milk in a mixing bowl and beat until thick and smooth. Spread over the cream cheese layer. Spread whipped topping over the pudding layer. Sprinkle with chopped nuts. Chill for 3 hours or longer.

Yield: 15 servings

Nancy Jackson, Product Sales

The Original Girl Scout Cookie

1 cup (2 sticks) butter or margarine, softened
1 cup sugar
2 eggs
2$1/2$ to 3 cups flour
2 teaspoons baking powder
1 teaspoon milk
1 teaspoon vanilla extract

Cream the butter and sugar in a mixing bowl until light and fluffy. Add the eggs and mix well. Add a mixture of the flour and baking powder and beat well. Stir in the milk and vanilla.

Chill thoroughly. Roll the dough into a log. Cut into $1/4$-inch slices. Place on an ungreased cookie sheet. Bake at 350 degrees for 8 to 10 minutes. Cool on a wire rack.

Yield: 2 to 3 dozen cookies

Note: The original cookies were sold 12 in a paper bag for 25 cents.

Message Cookies

4 egg whites
1 cup sugar
1/2 cup (1 stick) butter, melted
1/2 cup flour
2 tablespoons water
1/2 teaspoon vanilla extract or almond extract
1/4 teaspoon salt

Write 30 messages that will make others feel happy on little strips of paper and fold. Beat the egg whites in a mixing bowl until foamy. Gradually add the sugar and beat until soft peaks form. Add the butter, flour, water, vanilla and salt to the egg whites and beat until smooth.

Spread into 3-inch circles on a greased cookie sheet. Bake at 375 degrees for 8 minutes.

Place a folded message on each circle. Fold each cookie into thirds, then bend it gently in the center. Return the cookies to the oven if they become too hard to fold before filling all the cookies. Cool on a wire rack.

Yield: 30 cookies

Sherry Kelly, Communications Director

Fruitcake Cookies

6 tablespoons orange juice
1 teaspoon baking soda
3 eggs
3/4 cup (11/2 sticks) margarine, melted
1/4 cup honey
2 cups flour
1/2 cup sugar
1/2 cup packed brown sugar
1 pound diced dates
8 ounces candied cherries, chopped
8 ounces candied pineapple, chopped
3 cups chopped pecans

Combine the orange juice and baking soda in a large mixing bowl. Add the eggs, margarine and honey and mix well. Add a mixture of the flour, sugar and brown sugar and mix well. Stir in the dates, cherries, pineapple and pecans.

Drop by teaspoonfuls 2 inches apart onto a greased cookie sheet. Bake at 325 degrees for 12 to 15 minutes or until golden brown. Cool on a wire rack.

Yield: 50 cookies

Alta Hixon, Troop #29

Peanut Butter Cookies

1/2 cup shortening
1/2 cup sugar
1/2 cup packed brown sugar
1 egg
1/2 cup peanut butter
1 tablespoon water
1/2 teaspoon vanilla extract
1 cup sifted flour
11/2 teaspoons baking soda
1/4 teaspoon salt

Cream the shortening, sugar and brown sugar in a mixing bowl until light and fluffy. Add the egg, peanut butter, water and vanilla and mix well. Add a mixture of the flour, baking soda and salt and mix well. Roll into small balls.

Place 2 inches apart on a greased cookie sheet. Press with a fork dipped in flour. Bake at 325 degrees for 15 minutes. Cool on a wire rack.

Yield about 21/2 dozen cookies

Melissa Pigram, Troop #233

Peanut Butter Bites

¹/₂ cup sugar
¹/₂ cup corn syrup
1 cup peanut butter
2 cups crisp rice cereal

Bring the sugar and corn syrup to a boil in a saucepan over low heat. Remove from the heat. Stir in the peanut butter and rice cereal. Drop by teaspoonfuls onto waxed paper. Let stand until cool.

Yield: 12 cookies

Mary Kathryn Quigley, Troop #97

Simply Good Cookies

1 (2-layer) package butter pecan cake mix
1 (4-ounce) package butter pecan instant pudding mix
1 cup vegetable oil
1 egg
1 cup chopped pecans

Combine the cake mix, pudding mix, oil, egg and pecans in a bowl and mix well. Drop by teaspoonfuls 2 inches apart onto a greased cookie sheet. Bake at 350 degrees for 10 to 12 minutes or until golden brown. Cool on a wire rack.

Yield: 2 dozen cookies

Kiara Bass, Troop #234

Snickerdoodles

1 cup shortening
1 1/2 cups sugar
2 eggs
2 3/4 cups sifted flour
1 teaspoon baking soda
2 teaspoons cream of tartar
1/2 teaspoon salt
2 tablespoons cinnamon
2 tablespoons sugar

Cream the shortening and 1 1/2 cups sugar in a mixing bowl until light and fluffy. Add the eggs and beat well. Add a mixture of the flour, baking soda, cream of tartar and salt and mix well.

Chill thoroughly. Shape into walnut-size balls. Roll in a mixture of the cinnamon and 2 tablespoons sugar. Place 2 inches apart on an ungreased cookie sheet. Flatten slightly with a glass.

Bake at 400 degrees for 10 to 12 minutes. Cool on a wire rack.

Yield: 5 dozen cookies

Josephine Howard, Troop #97

Girl Scout Trivia
Girl Scouts have sold cookies since around 1912, but the first sale of commercially baked cookies took place in Philadelphia in 1936.

Carrot Oat Cookies

1/2 cup (1 stick) butter or margarine, softened
1/2 cup packed light brown sugar
1/4 cup sugar
1 egg
2 teaspoons grated orange zest
1 teaspoon vanilla extract
1 1/4 cups old-fashioned rolled oats
1/2 cup flour
1/4 cup wheat germ
1/4 cup dry milk powder
1 teaspoon baking powder
1/4 teaspoon salt
1 large carrot, shredded (about 1 cup)
3/4 cup raisins

Cream the butter, brown sugar and sugar in a mixing bowl until light and fluffy. Add the egg, orange zest and vanilla and mix well. Add a mixture of the rolled oats, flour, wheat germ, dry milk powder, baking powder and salt and mix well. Stir in the carrot and raisins. Drop by 2 tablespoonfuls 4 inches apart onto an ungreased cookie sheet. Flatten to 2-inch circles. Bake at 325 degrees for 12 to 14 minutes or until golden brown. Cool for 1 minute. Remove to a wire rack to cool completely.

Yield: 20 cookies

Desiree Orange, Troop #25

Oatmeal Raisin Cookies

1 cup (2 sticks) butter or margarine, softened
1 cup packed brown sugar
1/2 cup sugar
2 eggs
1 teaspoon vanilla extract
11/2 cups flour
1 teaspoon baking soda
1 teaspoon cinnamon
1/2 teaspoon salt (optional)
3 cups old-fashioned rolled oats
1 cup raisins

Cream the butter, brown sugar and sugar in a mixing bowl until light and fluffy. Add the eggs and vanilla and mix well. Add a mixture of the flour, baking soda, cinnamon and salt and mix well. Stir in the oats and raisins. Drop by rounded tablespoonfuls 2 inches apart onto an ungreased cookie sheet. Bake at 350 degrees for 10 to 12 minutes or until golden brown. Cool for 1 minute. Remove to a wire rack to cool completely.

Yield: 4 dozen cookies

Arja Thomas, Troop #25

Potato Chip Cookies

1 pound (4 sticks) butter, softened
1 cup sugar
2 teaspoons vanilla extract
3 cups sifted flour
1¹/₂ cups (5 ounces) finely crushed plain potato chips
Confectioners' sugar

Cream the butter and sugar in a mixing bowl until light and fluffy. Beat in the vanilla. Add the flour and mix well. Stir in the potato chips.

Drop by rounded teaspoonfuls 2 inches apart onto a greased cookie sheet. Bake at 325 degrees for 14 to 20 minutes.

Sprinkle the warm cookies with confectioners' sugar. Remove to a wire rack to cool completely.

Yield: 2 to 3 dozen cookies

Josephine Howard, Troop #97

Tea Cakes

1 cup (2 sticks) butter or margarine, softened
2 cups sugar
2 eggs
2 tablespoons milk
2 teaspoons vanilla extract
4 cups flour
1 teaspoon baking powder

Cream the butter and sugar in a mixing bowl until light and fluffy. Add the eggs, milk and vanilla and mix well. Add a mixture of the flour and baking powder and mix well.

Roll 1/8 inch thick on a floured surface. Cut with a cookie cutter. Place on a greased cookie sheet.

Bake at 350 to 400 degrees for 30 minutes. Cool on a wire rack.

Yield: 3 to 4 dozen cookies

Alexis Hicks, Troop #259

Icebox Cookies

1 1/2 cups shortening
2 cups packed brown sugar
3 eggs
1 tablespoon cinnamon
1 teaspoon baking soda
1 teaspoon cream of tartar
1 teaspoon vanilla extract
1/4 teaspoon salt
1/2 cup chopped nuts
5 cups flour

Cream the shortening and sugar in a mixing bowl until light and fluffy. Add the eggs and mix well. Add the cinnamon, baking soda, cream of tartar, vanilla, salt and nuts and mix well. Add the flour a little at a time, mixing well after each addition. Shape into 2 logs. Chill, tightly wrapped, in the refrigerator. Cut into 1/4-inch slices. Place on a greased cookie sheet. Bake at 425 degrees for 10 minutes. Cool on a wire rack.

Yield: 4 to 5 dozen cookies

Querrida Johnson, Troop #162

Chess Squares

1 (2-layer) package white or yellow cake mix
1/2 cup (1 stick) butter or margarine, melted
2 eggs
1/2 teaspoon vanilla extract
1 (8-ounce) package cream cheese, softened
1 (1-pound) package confectioners' sugar
1/2 teaspoon vanilla extract
2 eggs

Combine the cake mix, butter, eggs and vanilla in a bowl and mix well. Pat into a greased 9×13-inch cake pan, pressing partway up the sides.

Combine the cream cheese, confectioners' sugar, vanilla and eggs in a mixing bowl and mix for 3 minutes. Pour over the first layer.

Bake at 350 degrees for 35 to 40 minutes or until the middle is still gooey. Let stand for 2 hours or until set. Cut into squares.

Yield: 15 servings

Jeanne LeBlanc, Troop #39

One-Bowl Brownies

3/4 cup (11/2 sticks) butter, melted
1/4 cup baking cocoa
2 cups sugar
1 cup flour
3 eggs
1 teaspoon vanilla extract

Combine the butter and baking cocoa in a bowl and mix well. Add the sugar, flour, eggs and vanilla and mix well. Pour into a greased and floured 9×9-inch baking pan.

Bake at 350 degrees for 25 minutes or until a wooden pick inserted near the center comes out clean. Cool. Cut into squares.

Yield: 9 servings

Council Recipe

Blonde Brownies

1/2 cup (1 stick) margarine, melted
2 eggs
2 cups packed light brown sugar
1 teaspoon vanilla extract
11/2 cups flour
2 teaspoons baking powder
1/2 teaspoon salt
1 cup chopped nuts

Combine the margarine, eggs, brown sugar and vanilla in a mixing bowl and mix well. Add a mixture of the flour, baking powder and salt and mix well. Stir in the nuts.

Pour into a greased 9×13-inch baking pan. Bake at 350 degrees for 25 to 30 minutes. Cool. Cut into squares

Yield: 15 bars

Nancy Jackson, Product Sales Manager

Double Chocolate Chewies

1/2 cup (1 stick) butter, softened
1 (2-layer) package deluxe fudge cake mix
2 eggs
1 cup (6 ounces) semisweet chocolate chips
1 cup chopped nuts

Cream the butter in a mixing bowl until light and fluffy. Add the cake mix and eggs and mix well. Stir in the chocolate chips and nuts.

Pat into a greased 9×13-inch baking pan. Bake at 350 degrees for 20 to 30 minutes or until set. Cool. Cut into bars.

Yield: 15 bars

Lauren Sweajner, Troop #252

Chocolate Plum Thumbprints

1 cup chopped dried plums
1/4 cup sugar
1/2 cup water
1/2 cup chopped toasted walnuts
1/2 cup (3 ounces) semisweet chocolate chips
1 cup (2 sticks) margarine
11/2 cups packed brown sugar
2 cups flour
1/2 teaspoon baking soda
1/2 teaspoon salt
1/4 cup milk
2 cups quick-cooking oats

Combine the dried plums, sugar and water in a saucepan. Bring to a boil. Reduce the heat and simmer for 3 minutes, stirring constantly. Stir in the walnuts and chocolate morsels.

Cream the margarine and brown sugar in a mixing bowl until light and fluffy. Add a mixture of the flour, baking soda and salt a little at a time, beating well after each addition. Stir in the milk and oats. Shape into 11/4-inch balls. Place 2 inches apart on an ungreased cookie sheet. Make an indentation in each cookie with thumb. Bake at 350 degrees for 10 minutes. Fill the indentations with 1 teaspoon of the dried plum mixture. Bake for 2 to 3 minutes longer. Cool for 1 minute. Remove to a wire rack to cool completely.

Yield: 60 cookies

T'Kea Starks, Troop #259

Chocolate Macaroon Bars

1¹/₄ cups graham cracker crumbs
¹/₃ cup sugar
¹/₄ cup baking cocoa
¹/₃ cup butter or margarine, softened
1 (14-ounce) can sweetened condensed milk
1 (7-ounce) package flaked coconut
2 cups fresh white bread crumbs
2 eggs
2 teaspoons vanilla extract
1 cup (6 ounces) miniature semisweet
    chocolate chips

Combine the graham cracker crumbs, sugar, cocoa and butter in a bowl and mix well. Pat into a 9×13-inch cake pan. Bake at 350 degrees for 10 minutes. Combine the condensed milk, coconut, bread crumbs, eggs, vanilla and chocolate chips in a bowl and mix well. Spoon evenly over the baked crust. Bake at 350 degrees for 30 minutes or until golden brown. Cool. Cut into bars. Store, covered, in the refrigerator.

Yield: 24 to 36 bars

Nakyra Seaton, Troop #29

Chocolate Chip Cookie Bars

1/2 cup (1 stick) butter-flavor shortening
3/4 cup sugar
3/4 cup packed brown sugar
2 teaspoons vanilla extract
2 eggs
2 1/4 cups flour
1 teaspoon baking soda
1 teaspoon salt
2 tablespoons milk
2 cups (12 ounces) semisweet chocolate chips

Cream the shortening, sugar, brown sugar and vanilla in a mixing bowl until light and fluffy. Add the eggs 1 at a time, beating well after each addition. Add a mixture of the flour, baking soda and salt and mix well. Stir in the milk. Stir in the chocolate chips.

Pat into an ungreased 10×15-inch baking pan. Bake at 375 degrees for 20 minutes or until light brown. Cool. Cut into bars.

Yield: 12 to 15 bars

Kelsey Stephens, Troop #97

Salted Peanut Chews

1 (2-layer) package yellow cake mix
1/3 cup butter or margarine, softened
1 egg
3 cups miniature marshmallows
2/3 cup corn syrup
1/4 cup (1/2 stick) butter or margarine
2 teaspoons vanilla extract
1 (10-ounce) package peanut butter chips
2 cups crisp rice cereal
2 cups salted peanuts

Combine the cake mix, butter and egg in a mixing bowl. Beat at low speed until crumbly. Pat into an ungreased 9×13-inch baking pan. Bake at 350 degrees for 12 to 18 minutes or until light brown. Sprinkle with the marshmallows. Bake for for 1 to 2 minutes longer or until the marshmallows begin to puff. Let stand until cool.

Combine the corn syrup, butter, vanilla and peanut butter chips in a saucepan. Cook over low heat until smooth, stirring constantly. Stir in the rice cereal and peanuts. Spread evenly over the marshmallow layer. Chill for 1 hour or until firm. Cut into bars. Store in a tightly covered container.

Yield: 48 bars

Cleterria Grayer, Troop #29

Pralines

**2 cups packed light
  brown sugar
7 tablespoons
  evaporated milk**

**1 tablespoon butter
1 cup chopped pecans
1 teaspoon vanilla
  extract**

Combine the brown sugar, evaporated milk and butter in a saucepan and mix well. Bring to a boil, stirring constantly. Stir in the pecans. Cook, uncovered, over medium heat to 240 to 248 degrees on a candy thermometer, firm-ball stage. Remove from the heat. Add the vanilla and beat until thick and creamy. Drop by tablespoonfuls onto waxed paper. Let stand until cool.

Yield: 18 to 24 pralines

Dr. Mary Alice Cates, Executive Director of the Council

Easy Peach Cobbler

**6 tablespoons
  margarine
3/4 cup self-rising flour
3/4 cup sugar**

**3/4 cup milk
1 can sliced peaches
Cinnamon (optional)**

Melt the margarine in a 9×9-inch baking pan. Mix the flour, sugar and milk in a bowl. Pour over the melted margarine. Spoon the peaches over the flour mixture. Sprinkle with cinnamon. Bake at 350 degrees until the crust that forms is golden brown.

Yield: 4 to 6 servings

Mary Alston, Leader, Troop #139

Banana Pudding

1 (6-ounce) package vanilla instant pudding mix
1 (14-ounce) can sweetened condensed milk
1 (8-ounce) container whipped topping
7 or 8 bananas, sliced
1 package vanilla wafers

Prepare the pudding mix using the package directions. Fold in the condensed milk and whipped topping. Layer the bananas, vanilla wafers and pudding mixture in a serving bowl. Chill for 2 hours or longer.

Yield: 10 servings

Adrian Smith, Troop #97

Banana Pops

2 cups mashed bananas
1 cup orange juice
1 packet artificial sweetener
1 teaspoon lemon juice
1/4 cup water

Combine the bananas, orange juice, artificial sweetener, lemon juice and water in a bowl. Pour into six 4-ounce paper cups. Freeze until almost firm. Insert wooden skewers. Freeze until firm. Peel away the paper cups to serve.

Yield: 6 servings

Janet Young, Leader, Troop #7

Vanilla Custard

1/3 cup sugar
1 tablespoon flour
1 tablespoon cornstarch
1/4 teaspoon salt
11/2 cups milk
1 egg yolk, beaten
1 teaspoon vanilla extract

Combine the sugar, flour, cornstarch and salt in a saucepan. Stir in the milk and mix well. Cook over medium heat until thick and bubbly, stirring constantly. Cook for 3 minutes longer, stirring constantly.

Stir a small amount of the hot mixture into the beaten egg yolk; stir the egg yolk into the hot mixture.

Cook until the mixture comes to the boil, stirring constantly. Stir in the vanilla. Let stand until cool.

Yield: 3 to 4 servings

Dominique Meeks, Troop #128

Orange Sherbet

1 (2-liter) bottle orange-flavored soft drink
1 (14-ounce) can sweetened condensed milk

Combine the soft drink and condensed milk in a large bowl and mix well. Pour into an ice cream freezer container. Freeze using the manufacturer's directions.

Yield: 4 to 6 servings

Kay Davis, Carrollton Daisy Scouts

Fudgsicle Ice Cream

1/2 gallon chocolate milk
1 (14-ounce) can sweetened condensed milk
1 (12-ounce) container whipped topping

Combine the chocolate milk, condensed milk and whipped topping in a large bowl and mix well. Pour into an ice cream freezer container. Freeze using the manufacturer's directions.

Yield: 10 to 15 servings.

Kay Davis, Carrollton Daisy Scouts

Hot Fudge Sundae Sauce

4 ounces unsweetened chocolate, chopped
1/4 cup (1/2 stick) unsalted butter
2 tablespoons light corn syrup
1 cup sugar
3/4 cup heavy cream
1 teaspoon vanilla extract
1/8 teaspoon salt

Combine the chocolate, butter and corn syrup in a saucepan. Cook over medium-low heat for 3 to 4 minutes or until melted and smooth, stirring constantly. Add the sugar and cream. Cook for 2 minutes or until the sugar is dissolved, stirring constantly. Bring the sauce to a boil over medium heat. Boil for 8 minutes without stirring. Remove from the heat. Stir in the vanilla and salt. Spoon over ice cream.

Yield: 8 servings

Shalijah Harris, Troop #259

Snow Ice Cream

1 (14-ounce) can sweetened condensed milk
1 (5-ounce) can evaporated milk
Vanilla extract to taste
Clean snow
Cookies

Combine the condensed milk, evaporated milk and vanilla in a large mixing bowl and mix well. Beat in enough snow to reach a slushy consistency. Serve immediately with cookies.

Yield: 4 to 6 servings

Vanessa Wilson, Troop #252

Girl Scout Trivia
The newest and youngest Girl Scouts, known as Daisy Girl Scouts, started in 1984. Daisy Scouts are in kindergarten or first grade.

Praline Sauce

¹/₂ cup (1 stick) butter
1 cup packed brown sugar
1 cup milk
1 cup chopped pecans

Melt the butter in a saucepan. Stir in the brown sugar and milk. Cook over medium heat until the mixture comes to a boil and the sugar is dissolved, stirring constantly. Remove from the heat. Stir in the pecans. Serve over pound cake or ice cream.

Yield: 4 to 6 servings

Janet Young, Leader, Troop #7

Chocolate Syrup

2 cups sugar
2 tablespoons baking cocoa
1 tablespoon flour
1 cup milk
2 tablespoons margarine

Combine the sugar, baking cocoa and flour in a saucepan and mix well. Add the milk and margarine. Bring to a boil. Reduce the heat. Cook for 15 minutes or until of desired consistency, stirring frequently. Serve over plain cake.

Servings: 10 to 12 servings

Note: This is my great-grandmother's recipe.

Cari Brooke Canterbury, Troop #97

CEDAR POINT
PALETTE

A Gallery of Southern Recipes

Girl Scout Council of Northwest Mississippi
P.O. Box 1816
Greenwood, Mississippi 38935-1816
1-800-898-0535

Your Order	Qty	Total
Cedar Point Palette at $18.00 per book		$
Postage and handling at $2.50 per book		$
Gift wrap at $1.00 per book		$
	Total	$

Please make check payable to the Girl Scout Council of
Northwest Mississippi.

Name

Address

City   State   Zip

Photocopies will be accepted.